SELF-LEARNING MANAGEMENT SERIES

VIBRANT
PUBLISHERS

MICROECONOMICS ESSENTIALS

YOU ALWAYS WANTED TO KNOW

A go-to guide to understanding the building blocks
of Microeconomics

AMLAN RAY

Edited by **Arkadiusz Mironko**

Microeconomics Essentials You Always Wanted To Know

First Edition

Paperback ISBN 10: 1-63651-115-5
Paperback ISBN 13: 978-1-63651-115-3

Ebook ISBN 10: 1-63651-116-3
Ebook ISBN 13: 978-1-63651-116-0

Hardback ISBN 10: 1-63651-117-1
Hardback ISBN 13: 978-1-63651-117-7

Library of Congress Control Number: 2022938496

This publication is designed to provide accurate and authoritative information in regard to the subject matter covered. The Author has made every effort in the preparation of this book to ensure the accuracy of the information. However, information in this book is sold without warranty either expressed or implied. The Author or the Publisher will not be liable for any damages caused or alleged to be caused either directly or indirectly by this book.

Vibrant Publishers books are available at special quantity discount for sales promotions, or for use in corporate training programs. For more information please write to bulkorders@vibrantpublishers.com

Please email feedback / corrections (technical, grammatical or spelling) to spellerrors@vibrantpublishers.com

To access the complete catalogue of Vibrant Publishers, visit www.vibrantpublishers.com

SELF-LEARNING MANAGEMENT SERIES

TITLE	PAPERBACK* ISBN

ACCOUNTING, FINANCE & ECONOMICS

COST ACCOUNTING AND MANAGEMENT ESSENTIALS	9781636511030
FINANCIAL ACCOUNTING ESSENTIALS	9781636510972
FINANCIAL MANAGEMENT ESSENTIALS	9781636511009
MACROECONOMICS ESSENTIALS	9781636511818
MICROECONOMICS ESSENTIALS	9781636511153
PERSONAL FINANCE ESSENTIALS	9781636511849

ENTREPRENEURSHIP & STRATEGY

BUSINESS PLAN ESSENTIALS	9781636511214
BUSINESS STRATEGY ESSENTIALS	9781949395778
ENTREPRENEURSHIP ESSENTIALS	9781636511603

GENERAL MANAGEMENT

BUSINESS LAW ESSENTIALS	9781636511702
DECISION MAKING ESSENTIALS	9781636510026
LEADERSHIP ESSENTIALS	9781636510316
PRINCIPLES OF MANAGEMENT ESSENTIALS	9781636511542
TIME MANAGEMENT ESSENTIALS	9781636511665

*Also available in Hardback & Ebook formats

SELF-LEARNING MANAGEMENT SERIES

TITLE	PAPERBACK* ISBN

HUMAN RESOURCE MANAGEMENT

TITLE	PAPERBACK* ISBN
DIVERSITY IN THE WORKPLACE ESSENTIALS	9781636511122
HR ANALYTICS ESSENTIALS	9781636510347
HUMAN RESOURCE MANAGEMENT ESSENTIALS	9781949395839
ORGANIZATIONAL BEHAVIOR ESSENTIALS	9781636510378
ORGANIZATIONAL DEVELOPMENT ESSENTIALS	9781636511481

MARKETING & SALES MANAGEMENT

TITLE	PAPERBACK* ISBN
DIGITAL MARKETING ESSENTIALS	9781949395747
MARKETING MANAGEMENT ESSENTIALS	9781636511788
SALES MANAGEMENT ESSENTIALS	9781636510743
SERVICES MARKETING ESSENTIALS	9781636511733

OPERATIONS & PROJECT MANAGEMENT

TITLE	PAPERBACK* ISBN
AGILE ESSENTIALS	9781636510057
OPERATIONS & SUPPLY CHAIN MANAGEMENT ESSENTIALS	9781949395242
PROJECT MANAGEMENT ESSENTIALS	9781636510712
STAKEHOLDER ENGAGEMENT ESSENTIALS	9781636511511

*Also available in Hardback & Ebook formats

About the Author

Prof. Amlan Ray is currently Senior Director & Dean at SRISIIM, New Delhi, a management and research Institution recognized by the Ministry of Science & Technology and Ministry of Education, Government of India. He has 27 years of experience working in Corporates, Consulting, Training, and Academia.

His corporate experience and research area lie in Economic Analysis, Digital Transformation, and International Business. He is also an advisor to Infinite Sum Modelling Inc., a US-based multinational consulting firm in the area of International Trade. Amlan has also authored several articles in Management and Economics journals.

Amlan has executed various training and consulting assignments sponsored by organizations like the AICTE, World Bank, PHD Chamber of Commerce, Grafoventure (Italy), Master Card Foundation, and Data Science Network (Nigeria). He has been instrumental in designing National Occupational Standard (NOS) in the area of Digital Transformation for National Skill Development Corporation (NSDC), India.

Amlan is a B.Tech., MBA, M.A. (Economics) and has submitted his Ph.D. thesis at Amrita Viswa Vidyapeetham, India in the area of International Trade.

Other contributors

We would like to thank our editor, **Arkadiusz Mironko** for his contribution to making this book the best version possible. Arkadiusz is an assistant professor of management and entrepreneurship at Indiana University East, School of Business and Economics. Previously, he worked at the Rotterdam School of Management Erasmus University in the Netherlands, and the AGSM at the University of California, Riverside. His core research interests are in the area of business strategy, global economic competition, and knowledge creation and transfer through R&D between multinational corporations entering developing economies and collaboration with indigenous firms. Mironko is the author of the book Determinants of FDI Flows within Emerging Economies: A Case Study of Poland, published by Palgrave Macmillan, several journal articles and book chapters. Arkadiusz received his Ph.D. in International Business Strategy from Rutgers University.

What experts say about this book!

Microeconomics Essentials is a must-read for anyone looking for a solid foundation in microeconomics as it is presented in an easy-to-understand fashion. Student learning is enhanced with a variety of real-world applications of the material. The book can be used as a primary text in undergraduate microeconomics classes or as a useful supplement to more advanced courses.

– Richard Roberts, Professor of Economics and Finance,

Monmouth University, USA

This book explains in a brief and concise way by avoiding too many technicalities and focusing mostly on concepts that could be applied in real life. This book could be used as an introductory book for undergraduate students or even MBA students who do not have any background in business and/ economics. The end-of-chapter summaries and questions are easy and straightforward and are good reviews of the basics of the chapter.

– Indrit Hoxha, Associate Professor of Economics,

Penn State Harrisburg School of Business Administration, USA

Conceptually simple and pedagogically sound, this introductory textbook is meant for beginners and under-graduate students from Management, Commerce and other disciplines. It provides detailed insights into the basics of Micro Economics thereby equipping students with a working knowledge of the subject.

– Dr Partha Pratim Sahu, Centre for Good Governance and Policy

Analysis (CGGPA), NIRDPR

What experts say about this book!

For a beginner, this book gives comprehensive coverage of all topics that they need to learn. The present NEP curriculum on economics will find this book a great facilitator. The layout and font of the book are perfect and standardised. The Self-Learning Management series is pioneering and trendsetting. This series has the caliber to become a best-seller series! This book is brimming with information starting from basic to advanced topics of microeconomics. An economics faculty will greatly benefit from this book, as this book provides insights into theoretical and practical challenges. This book dwells on the vision of "know-hows" for lifelong learning.

– Prof Clement D Souza, Dean, School of Humanities,

St Joseph's University, Bangalore, India

Microeconomics Essentials is an approachable description and analysis, written keeping in mind students beginning economics from scratch at college or university. A clear, readable text is supported by data-responsive material, numerical, and multiple-choice questions to check a learner's understanding. Attention is paid to both traditional and modern ways of looking at microeconomics and has been carefully discussed to show how they can be used to discuss economic problems.

– Prof. S.S.Somra, Department of Economics,

University of Rajasthan, India

What experts say about this book!

This book can be hailed as a textbook since the entire subject matter has clarity of exposition and its simple, empirical, and graphical presentation of topics will be easy to understand. A summary at the end of chapters is a good way to recapitulate information. Undergraduate students or anyone who is interested to understand the behaviour of an individual, firm, etc. will find this book useful. This book can be used in courses like BA Economics, BBA, and BCom. Starting with basic concepts, this book is written concisely yet comprehensively. This is an ideal book to help you to grasp the essentials of economics quickly and easily even if you're a novice.

– Dr.S.Padma Annakamu, Assistant Professor,

Department of Economics, PSGRKCW, India

This page is intentionally left blank

Table of Contents

10 International Trade 183

Preface

Economics has influenced policymaking across the globe, and the world of finance and trade is completely dependent on this subject. Despite the tremendous practical application of the subject, it is often perceived as obscure and theoretical. This book attempts to make the readers understand the practicalities of the subject of Economics. Examples taken from various industries in this book demonstrate the application part. The book tries to acquaint the readers with the practical applications of microeconomics, unraveling each aspect of economics jargon. At the end of the book, the reader should be able to appreciate the practical application of microeconomics in business and policymaking. The purpose of the book is to make people without an economics background comfortable with the subject. As a learning outcome, the readers should be able to appreciate business articles comfortably or be able to engage in discussions on economic issues after reading the book. The book will help students of Economics at the undergraduate level and in executive MBA programs to follow and understand their academic curriculum better.

This page is intentionally left blank

Introduction to the book

The world of trade and finance are dependent on the economic sciences. The knowledge of economics is essential for students and professionals who want to make career in the world of business. Usage of big data and computers have given the economic sciences the capacity to forecast with fair amount of accuracy. The importance of economic sciences has made it essential for students and professionals to have fair idea about elementary economics to fulfil their career aspirations. However, often Economics text books are found to be theoretical and full of jargons which are difficult to follow. This book attempts to simplify various microeconomic theories and explain the various terms used in economics with examples from business world. Discussion of different theories in this book makes it easier for the readers to understand the application of economics in various fields. The book introduces the readers with core concepts of economics like demand and supply and take them through theories of consumer choice, market, factors of production and finally international economics. At the end of the book, the readers will be able to appreciate following concepts of microeconomics:

- Concept of scarcity and choice

- Law of demand and supply

- Price elasticity of demand and supply

- Consumer behaviour with both cardinal and ordinal utility theory

- Theory of cost and production

- Various forms of market ranging from monopoly to perfect competition

- Concepts of revenue, cost and profit

- Overview of factors of production

- Basics of trade including free trade and trade barriers

Finally, the readers will be able to understand how different economic theories affect our day to day life and determine public policies at national and global level.

Who can benefit from the book?

- Undergraduate students can use this as a text book that covers their syllabus

- Students at master's level in programmes like MBA, often join from non- economics background. This book will be useful for them to understand basics of economics

- Business professionals can use this to understand decision making in the companies and industries

- Entrepreneurs will be benefitted by learning the basics of microeconomics to understand policy matters

This page is intentionally left blank

How to use this book?

The book can be used in multiple ways depending on the need of the reader. The book focuses on explaining various microeconomics concepts with examples from business and day to day life.

- Students can use this to understand basics of economics

- This can be used as a reference book by various UG level students like engineering etc. to understand the concept of economics and its application in industry. Students will benefit when they will try to match the theories with their practical learning

- The readers may conduct small survey, experiments to check empirically theories like law of demand etc. discussed in the book

- Students may prepare graphs, diagrams with various economics databases available with World Bank, CIA Fact Book etc. and check the application of economic theories

- Entrepreneurs may use this to understand basics of microeconomics and complement the book with policy papers and strategic documents

This page is intentionally left blank

Chapter **1**

Fundamentals of Economics

This chapter introduces the readers to the fundamentals of Economics. Economics is one of the most important aspects of social science and is used immensely in policymaking. The application of economics improves the quality of life across the globe. But often, we are not clear about the fundamental concepts of economics. The purpose of this chapter is to bring about clarity on the need, use, and concepts of economics before entering into a detailed discussion on various topics of microeconomics in the subsequent chapters.

Key learning objectives of this chapter include the reader's understanding of the following:

- The importance of studying economics

- The definition of economics

- The importance of concepts like scarcity and choice

- The difference between microeconomics and macroeconomics

1.1 Why Study Economics?

People study Economics for various purposes: to attain a good job, for the purpose of higher education, or just to gather knowledge. But studying economics can be even more purposeful. It enables us to make rational decisions. The decision to choose the political party that will formulate policies keeping our interests in mind, the decision to choose the job that will give more returns, or choosing to buy the stock which is the best investment option, are all decisions that Economics can help us make.

We hear a lot of terms without understanding their intrinsic meaning. We hear about monetary policy, credit squeeze, and financial inclusiveness. However, our understanding is often superficial. To appreciate these terms, we need an understanding of economics. We hear about the taxation policy of the Biden Government or the tariff imposed by the European Union on US imports from China. The study of Economics enables us to appreciate the debates and discussions on these topics.

Everyone is interested in learning about vibrant business environments, stable job markets with low unemployment, and the growth in the country's economy. Knowledge of economics allows us to understand the factors that affect the business environment or the job market. It also makes us think about the policy measures which can achieve these objectives.

We know that for investing in the stock market, we need to have information not only about the companies we are interested in but also about the economy and the events affecting the stock market. The study of economics enables us to read and comprehend a business newspaper. The study of economics improves the analytical capability and business acumen needed for success in a profession.[1]

Economics expands our vocabulary, allows us to put new terms into practice, makes us understand our own spending habits, leverage economic tools, and improves our career prospects.[2]

An engineer needs an understanding of economics to make the right decision for controlling production costs, while a human resource manager with a knowledge of economics can optimize the utilization of the workforce. With economics, a doctor will know which segment of patients will be able to afford a particular line of treatment. Thus, economics can be applied and utilized in various fields of operation

Finally, economics makes us realize the fact that resources are scarce. Optimum utilization of these scarcely available goods can make our life better and improve our standards of living.

1. Lindholm, R. W. (1944). The Development of a Scientific Attitude in Economics. The American Journal of Economics and Sociology, 3(2), 239–250.

2. Chladek, N. (2017, November 30). 7 REASONS WHY YOU SHOULD STUDY ECONOMICS. Harvard Business School Online. https://online.hbs.edu/blog/post/5-reasons-why-you-should-study-economics

1.2 Defining Economics

Samuelson and Nordhaus define[3] economics as the study of how societies use scarce resources to produce valuable goods and services and distribute them among different individuals.

As per the Economist,[4] The most concise definition of economics is the study of how society uses its scarce resources.

So, economics deals with the optimum utilization of the resources that are scarce in nature. This is applicable to an individual as well. A salaried person needs to budget for different needs within his monthly income. He needs to allocate funds for gasoline, food, and rent, as well as funds for entertainment. There needs to be a provision for savings as a means of social security during rainy days.

Webster's Dictionary[5] defines optimization as a process that tries to make something as effective as possible. A household tries to make its expenditure as effective as possible. The way a household tries to minimize their running costs per month and maximize utility for the family members with a limited income is optimization. This optimization is done assuming that the consumer knows what is best for him. He is rational and his decisions are based on logic. When we aggregate the individual needs, we hit upon the societal needs.[6]

---

3. Samuelson, P. A., & Nordhaus, W. D. (2009). Economics 19e.p 1.

4. The Economist, Economics A-Z terms. https://www.economist.com/economics-a-to-z/a

5. Dictionary, M. W. (2002). Merriam-webster. On-line at http://www. mw. com/home. htm, 14.

6. Hossain, F. A., & Ali, M. K. (2014). Relation between individual and society. Open Journal of Social Sciences, 2(08), 130.

A country needs to budget funds for its defense, its infrastructure, healthcare, and education for its citizens. These are planned with the limited or scarce resources it receives through various means of revenue, in particular the taxes collected by the state.[7]

If resources were not scarce, the basic premises of economics would have been challenged, as we always assume that wealth is limited.[8] In the next section, we deal in detail with the concept of scarcity.

1.3 Concept of Scarcity

If we had Aladdin's Genie's lamp and could have anything and everything we wanted, then there would be no problem of scarcity. Unfortunately, despite the rapid evolution of humankind and human society, most resources are still scarce in this world. Neither the individual nor the state has any magical lamp to solve the problem of hunger and poverty. Moreover, human needs or wants are unlimited.[9] So, even if we solve the problem of poverty and most people gain access to food, clothing, and shelter, the problem of scarcity will not be over. Herein lies the need for economics.

Economics is concerned about using scarce resources optimally for producing valuable goods and services. Then, it takes on the onus of distributing these scarce resources among different

---

7. Blinder, A. S., & Solow, R. M. (1973). Does fiscal policy matter?. Journal of public economics, 2(4), 319-337.

8. Pilzer, P. Z., & Davie, K. (1994). Unlimited wealth. New York: Crown.

9. Samuelson, P. A., & Nordhaus, W. D. (2009). Economics 19e.p 1

individuals. So, it has the dual task of production and distribution. Economics tries to answer three basic questions: *what to produce, how to produce, and for whom to produce?* These are also called the central problems of an economy.

The concept of scarcity is prevalent at an individual level as well as a societal level. Alice wants to go on a vacation to Switzerland, but she cannot. She needs to settle her EMI[10] on her car loan, which leaves her with fewer savings to plan a vacation. Her needs and wants far exceed her monthly income.

On a societal level, a country wants to spend more money on education, healthcare, and universal basic income for all. But the country may be compelled to spend on defense, service its debt from the International Monetary Fund (IMF), and may also need to spend money on building infrastructure. Despite its good intentions, the Secretary of the Treasury is not able to allocate more money to areas like education or healthcare. Thus, the need for optimization arises. The country's socio-economic policies should lead to optimum utilization of scarce resources, which will be the best option for its citizens.

Land, labor, capital, and entrepreneurship are **factors of production**. Factors of production are also scarce, and hence, the manufacturing sector needs to utilize scarce resources to maximize its productivity and minimize its cost of operation. Scarcity forces us to make a choice, more specifically, a rational choice, which is an important area of decision-making in economics. The concept of choice is explained in the next section.

---

10. EMI is an Equal Monthly Instalment set by a bank or financial institution against a loan.

1.4 The Concept of Choice

Scarcity leads to the problem of choice. As incomes are limited, one needs to limit one's consumption and spend money only on selected items. Scarcity determines the choice in the above scenario and leads the individual to make the decision that will benefit him or her the most. Economists study the behavior of consumers, and choices made by people as a part of the decision-making process.[11] When resources are scarce, people need to make their choices judiciously. When we have limited capital and labor to produce a limited amount of goods and services, we need to make a choice regarding what to produce.

Again, we need to choose how much to produce from the limited availability of capital and labor. If labor is available in abundance in a particular society, it may opt for a labor-intensive industry. Countries like China or India, which have abundant manpower, might prefer a labor-intensive industry. But Finland, a country with just 5.5 million people, may not find labor-intensive industries suitable for it. While Finland may have less manpower, it might have an abundant supply of capital available in the country. It may focus on technology-driven, capital-intensive industries.

While countries with abundant labor may opt for industries like footwear or garments, a country with cheaply available capital may opt for high-tech electronic industries or focus on robotics, for example.

---

11. Dorothy Noyes. (2015). Fairy-Tale Economics: Scarcity, Risk, Choice. Narrative Culture, 2(1), 1–26.

Next comes the choice of distribution. How can one distribute whatever is produced in society among various stakeholders? Capitalism and the market economy make this less complicated; it produces for the people who have money or purchasing power. Purchasing power determines *for whom to produce.*[12] In socialist economies, they produce for the people who need the goods the most, but this idea may appear utopian and so far, does not have strong evidence of successful implementation.[13]

Opportunity cost is a concept in economics that makes us choose between various opportunities. For example, while you are reading this book, you are missing the opportunity to watch a movie. The opportunity cost of reading this book may be the loss of an hour spent watching a movie. Opportunity cost is the value of the next best alternative that we forego. Let's look at another example: Tom got two job offers after completing his graduation. One at P&G with an income of $70,000 per year, the other one at Ford with an income of $60,000 per year; he decides to go for the P&G job offer. Now, the opportunity cost of his choice is $60,000 which he could get out of the next best alternative.

The concepts of scarcity, choice, and opportunity cost are fundamental to the discussion of economics and many of the theories are based on these concepts.

---

12. Samuelson, P. A., & Nordhaus, W. D. (2009). Economics 19e.p 60

13. Lipset, S. M., & Bence, G. (1994). Anticipations of the Failure of Communism. Theory and Society, 23(2), 169–210.

1.5 Microeconomics and Macroeconomics

In present days, Economics is categorized into two subfields; Microeconomics and Macroeconomics. Adam Smith is considered to be the father of Microeconomics. The terms microeconomics and macroeconomics were first used by a Norwegian economist Ragnar Frisch in 1933 in his paper Propagation Problems and Impulse Problem in Dynamic Economics, published in the book Economic Essays in Honour of Gustav Cassel, (London, Frank Cass & Co.,1933)[14] The modern form of Macroeconomics came into existence with the publication of John Maynard Keynes' revolutionary General Theory of Employment, Interest, and Money in 1936[15].

Microeconomics studies economic phenomena at the individual level. Microeconomics shows how individuals make their purchasing decisions. It shows how consumer decisions affect demand and supply. The interaction between buyers and sellers and the related decisions of purchase and production are dealt with in microeconomics. It shows how the prices are determined in the market according to the interaction of buyers and sellers. It also deals with the cost, production, revenue, and profit of individual firms that constitute the industry. A liberal regime may choose to cut taxes on various goods and services sold in an economy. An easy interpretation of this choice could be a loss of revenue for the government due to the tax cut. But in reality, often it is found that a tax cut leads to greater purchases and does not impact government revenue adversely. There could even be an increase in the tax collection due to the sale of a greater

14. Dwivedi, D. N. (2016). Microeconomics: Theory and Applications. Vikas Publishing House.

15. Samuelson, P. A., & Nordhaus, W. D. (2009). Economics 19e.p 5

number of units. Microeconomic analysis enables policy decisions to be made. Taxation policies may be part of macroeconomic policies but their inherent mechanism depends on microeconomic theories.

Microeconomic theories are often able to establish a cause-and-effect relationship between various economic factors. This enables the prediction of future events, like estimating future market demand or a commodity price. These predictions may often be conditional and inaccurate, like weather predictions but still, add immense value to the discourse of economics.

Microeconomic theories, particularly price theories, help in business decision-making. It enables firms to adopt revenue models based on price theories and companies to adopt strategies for increasing their market share or reducing their operational loss.

Most importantly, microeconomic theories provide the basis for formulations that maximize social welfare. It enables addressing issues that create inefficiency, reduced production, and reduced consumption in society.

Macroeconomics, on the other hand, deals with the economy as a whole, at the national level or at the global level. It is concerned about aggregate demand, supply, savings, income, and expenditure at the national or global level. It provides inputs for policymaking at the national level. The concerns of employment, production, and productivity are addressed by macroeconomics. It suggests taxation policies or monetary policies. The country's total income is calculated by the GDP (Gross Domestic Product) and a year-on-year change in income is termed as the growth of the economy. The issues related to GDP or growth are, therefore, related to macroeconomics. While in microeconomics, we are concerned about the income of a single farmer, for example, in macroeconomics, we analyze the income of the entire agricultural sector. While we study the performance of an individual company like Ford in microeconomics, we study the entire automobile industry under macroeconomics. Macroeconomics is essential in making decisions about the country's income and expenditure strategy and its taxation policy. These policies are termed fiscal policies. Monetary policy also falls under the study of macroeconomics, where we analyze the supply of money, possible interest rates, industry's requirements for credit, etc. At a global level, we follow the multi-country trade system.

The focus of this book is on microeconomics. In the following chapters, we will deal with problems of the economy at the individual level. A thorough understanding of microeconomics will help us in decision-making at the individual level.

Discussion Questions

1. Economics has its utility in a situation where we have scarcity. When the earth will have surplus wealth compared to its needs, what can be the utility of Economics?

2. Analyze a few applications of microeconomics in business.

Chapter Summary

♦ Economics improves our decision-making capability at an aggregate as well as at the individual level.

♦ Economics allows us to understand, debate and analyze various policy decisions made by the Government.

♦ An engineer, a doctor, and an HR Manager will equally benefit from knowing the concepts of economics.

♦ Economics is the study of how society uses its scarce resources.

♦ The scarcity of resources is the main reason behind the evolution of the subject of economics.

♦ For optimum utilization of scarce resources, rational choices need to be made.

♦ The central problems of an economy are what to produce, how to produce, and for whom to produce?

♦ Microeconomics studies economic phenomena at the individual level.

♦ Macroeconomics deals with the economy as a whole at the national level or at the global level.

Quiz

1. **Economics helps us in understanding the following, except**

    a. Government policies

    b. Business decisions

    c. Making decisions related to personal finance

    d. Negotiating real estate brokerage

2. **The central problems of an economy are _____.**

    a. scarcity and choice

    b. choice and consumer preference

    c. what, how and for whom to produce

    d. money and taxation

3. **The reason behind the evolution of the subject of economics is _____.**

    a. money

    b. growth of the economy

    c. business applications

    d. scarcity

4. **Alice leaves her job at P&G with a monthly salary of $6000 for a partnership in a firm with earning potential of $10000. The opportunity cost of her decision is:**

    a. $10000

    b. $6000

    c. $4000

    d. $5000

5. **A Country with abundant human resources is likely to choose an industry that is _____.**

    a. capital intensive

    b. technology-intensive

    c. labor-intensive

    d. none of the above

6. **A country like Norway will have an advantage in _____ .**

    a. capital intensive industry

    b. labor-intensive industry

    c. agriculture

    d. manufacturing

7. **Scarcity of resources is experienced by _____.**

   a. individuals

   b. households

   c. state

   d. all of the above

8. **Purchasing behavior of a consumer is studied in _____.**

   a. Microeconomics

   b. Macroeconomics

   c. Developmental Economics

   d. None of the above

9. **Fiscal policy is studied in_____.**

   a. Macroeconomics

   b. Microeconomics

   c. behavioral Economics

   d. Environmental Economics

10. The recent pandemic has impacted global growth and the forecasts are carried out by economists with a specialization in _____.

   a. Macroeconomics

   b. Microeconomics

   c. Both of the above

   d. None of the above

Answers	1 – a	2 – c	3 – d	4 – b	5 – c
	6 – a	7 – d	8 – a	9 – a	10 – a

This page is intentionally left blank

Chapter **2**

Demand and Supply

This chapter introduces the readers to the law of demand and supply which is at the center of microeconomic theories. In this chapter, we will discuss, in detail, the concepts of demand and supply, construct a demand and supply schedule, and derive the required curves out of these. We will also analyze how the equilibrium point is reached and how prices are determined.

The purpose of this chapter is to create a clear understanding of the economic phenomenon of demand and supply and enable readers to appreciate various economic theories and their applications in the subsequent chapters.

Key learning objectives of this chapter include the reader's understanding of the following:

- Understanding the law of demand and supply
- Understanding how the equilibrium point is obtained

- Learning how the price points are determined

- Studying the graphical representation of demand and supply schedule

- Discovering how the demand and supply curves can shift

- Understanding various types of goods like normal goods, essential consumer goods, inferior goods, and luxury goods

2.1 Demand and Supply

The law of supply and demand is at the center of economic theories. Most economic phenomena are explained using the concept of demand and supply of various goods and services. This law explains the demand and supply of various goods and commodities as well as the factors of production like labor and capital.

A piece of news dated January 12, 2022, has the tagline 'Food prices up, shelves empty'[16]. It blames the pandemic-related workers' absence that has created food shortages and warns about high inflation. The news report states that the price of new cars went up during the last year by 11.8 %, and groceries were dearer by 6.3%. Chicken and fish prices jumped by 10.4% and 8.4 % respectively. How does one explain these changes in price? In the

16. Davidson, P. (2022, January 12). Inflation reaches highest level since 1982 as consumer prices jump 7% in 2021. USA Today. https://www.usatoday.com/ story/money/2022/01/12/cpi-2021-consumer-prices-climbed-7-2021-fastest-pace-since-1982/9178235002/

economic environment, there is a robust theory called the 'theory of supply and demand'[17] which explains the inside story behind these shifts in price. The theory of demand and supply explains how there can be a shift in consumer demand due to reasons like consumer preference and income level. It also shows how the production cost determines the supply of various materials. Production costs are determined by the prevailing wages, raw material costs, cost of electricity, and many other production-related factors. Supply is also dependent on the competitors' prices, prevailing taxes, transportation costs, etc. Tax rebates may also boost supply. On the other hand, production costs may come down when there is a cheap import of raw materials and intermediate goods.

The interaction of demand and supply in the *marketplace* determines the price. Now, what is a marketplace? A marketplace is a place or area where buyers and sellers meet. The idea of a physical place is becoming obsolete, as the buyers and sellers can now meet virtually. So, a market is a platform for the interaction of buyers and sellers. The market is also a mechanism that allows the interaction of buyers and sellers to determine the demand, supply, and resultant price.

Conceptually, **demand** is a desire for a good backed by the purchasing power and willingness to pay. **Purchasing power** is the ability of the customer to pay for the goods. For example, Yasmin is an established businesswoman and for a long time, she has had a desire to buy a fancy sports car. She can afford to pay for it. But whenever she plans to buy the car, some other priorities come to her mind and she postpones the purchase of the fancy car. She has the desire along with the ability to pay for the car but lacks the willingness to pay for it. Her desire for the car is

---

17. Samuelson, P. A., & Nordhaus, W. D. (2009). Economics 19e.p 54

not a demand, but a potential demand. Desire without sufficient purchasing power is merely a wish. For qualifying as effective demand, the desire needs to be complemented by the ability and the willingness to pay for the good or service.

Individual demand is defined as the quantity an individual person buys during a specified period, say per day, per week, or per month. Market demand constitutes the aggregated demand of all the users of a product during a specified time. It is the sum of all the individual demands.

The Law of Demand:

The law of demand explains the relationship between the quantity demanded and the price of a commodity. Although the quantity demanded of a commodity depends on various factors such as the consumer's tastes, income, price of the substitutes, advertisement, branding, etc., price is considered to be the most important determinant of demand.

The law of demand states that all other things remaining constant, the quantity demanded of a commodity increases when the price decreases and decreases when the price increases[18]. This shows that demand is inversely proportional to the price and decreases with an increase in price. The law is applicable in a state called ceteris paribus, i.e., all other things remaining unchanged. So, when we consider the effect of price on demand, we assume there is no change in the consumer's income, tastes, and preferences, price of substitute products, or advertising budget of the product.

---

18. Salvatore, Dominick. Schaum's Outline of Microeconomics, 4th edition. McGraw-Hill, 2006.P.14.

There are four interpretations of the laws of supply and demand:

i.   If the supply increases and the demand remains the same, the price will fall.

ii. If the supply decreases and the demand remains the same, the price will rise.

iii. If the supply remains the same and demand goes up, the price will rise.

iv. If the supply remains the same and demand goes down, the price will fall.

Suppose the supply of shrimp goes up in the market due to increased imports from India and Vietnam, but the demand remains the same as there is no change in the population or their tastes, eventually, the price of shrimp will drop. Contrary to this, if the supplies are restricted or stopped, the price will go up as the demand remains the same.

During winter, consumption of meat and poultry increases, while the supply remains the same, thereby increasing the price. In another situation where the supply of red meat remains the same in the market, but buyers do not prefer red meat due to health concerns, the buyers' preference has an adverse effect on the price.

Similarly, as Easter arrives in spring for the majority of Americans, it is the time for packing Easter baskets and buying lots of chocolates. It is a big business time for chocolate sellers and due to the increasing demand, the price of chocolates also goes up. In this case, both the demand and supply have gone up. But the relative increase in demand is more than the increase in supply, which leads to an increase in price.

In a market economy, the buyers or consumers constitute the demand side of the market, while the producers or sellers constitute the supply side of the market.

Similar to the concept of individual demand and market demand, in the theory of supply, market supply equals the supply of individual firms or producers in the economy. For example, soaps and shampoos are manufactured by big MNCs like Unilever, Procter & Gamble, and Loreal. There are numerous other manufacturers too. Hence, the supply side of the market comprises the total shampoo sales by Unilever, P&G, Loreal, and numerous other manufacturers in a specific market, say the U.K. market.

Demand Schedule

From the work of economist Alfred Marshall[19], it is understood that a fall in price will increase the quantity demanded. Below, a demand schedule has been constructed with the demand for washing powder boxes in a local city market (per month).

Table 2.1   Demand Schedule of Washing powder

Price in USD ($) per pound	Total no. of packs of 1 pound (in'000) per week
12	100
10	110
8	125
6	150
4	180

19. Brown, D. J., & Calsamiglia, C. (2014). Alfred Marshall's cardinal theory of value: the strong law of demand. Economic Theory Bulletin, 2(1), 65-76.

The above table perfectly follows the law of demand. The consumption of washing powder stands at 100,000 pounds per month when the average price of washing powder is $12 per pound. The price falls to $10, increasing the demand to 110,000 pounds. When the suppliers reduce the price further to $8, the city's washing powder consumption goes up by 125,000 pounds. The suppliers of washing powder do not stop there. Maybe, their cost of production has gone down due to new technology used or the distributors receiving cheaper imports from Asia. The price falls further to $6 and $4 per pound during the next two months. This takes the demand to a new high of 150,000 pounds, followed by reaching the 180,000-pound mark.

Now, when the above demand schedule is represented graphically, the demand curve is derived. Figure 2.1 represents the demand curve.

Figure 2.1 **Demand Curve of Washing Powder**

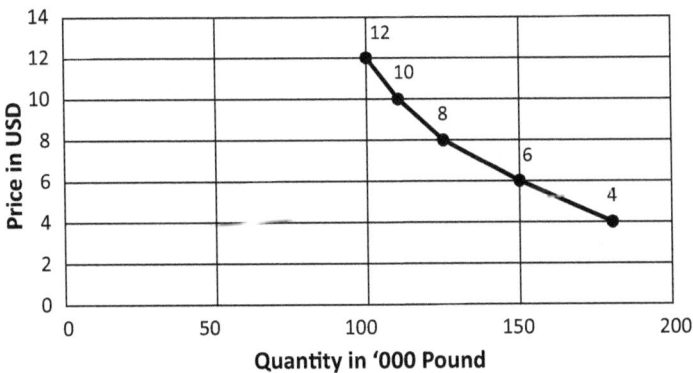

The law of demand is an empirical fact. When the prices of cell phones were high and people were charged for incoming calls, only a few people had cell phones; however, now almost everyone has access to cell phones. Personal computers were a luxury a few decades back, but the falling price has multiplied their sales.

The above curve slopes downward to the right. What are the reasons behind this? The most common causes for the increase in demand during a fall in price are the substitution effect and income effect.

Substitution effect

When a particular good becomes expensive, a rational consumer will purchase other cheaper goods to replace it. If product A becomes expensive and there are substitutes X, Y, Z at a cheaper price; the consumer will substitute A with X, Y, Z. If the price of pork goes up, the consumer will consume less pork and buy more chicken, as the chicken will now be cheaper compared to pork.

Income effect

When the price of a commodity falls, the real income of people goes up. In contrast, if the price goes up, the real income of people goes down, making them relatively poorer. The rise in real income makes individuals purchase more in general, and purchase the product with the reduced price in particular.

Exceptions to the Law of Demand

Though the law of demand is a fundamental law of economics, there are exceptions to the law of demand in the case of certain goods and situations.

1. **Speculative goods** – There are certain goods in which an increase in price, creates expectations of a further price rise. In the stock market, when the stock price goes up, there are more buyers of the stock, as they anticipate a further rise in price. The same is applicable to real estate prices or the price of gold. Contrary to these, a falling price may create an impression that there will be a further fall in the price. Investors panic in a falling market and assume that they will be better off selling their stocks, as the market prices may decline further.

2. **Luxury goods** – There is a 'snob value' associated with certain products, and rich people prefer purchasing these, one of the inherent reasons being that they are out of reach of most consumers. A rare painting, a designer suit, or a precious ornament is valued because of its high price. Here, a lower price may not attract more buyers.

3. **Giffen goods.** An exception to the law of demand is Giffen goods, named after Sir Robert Giffen[20] (1837-1910). It was observed in Ireland that when the main consumption items of food were meat and potato, people bought even more potatoes despite the increase in potato price and there was a corresponding fall in the meat prices. Suppose bread prices go up, while butter prices fall. There will now be a price difference between butter and bread. Poor people will curtail their budget on butter and spend the money on bread to manage within budget.

---

20. Dwivedi, D. N. (2016). Microeconomics: Theory and Applications.p.39. Vikas Publishing House.

Law of Supply

The law of supply states *that the supply of a product goes up with the increase in price and goes down with a decrease in its price, other things remaining constant.* It indicates that price and supply are positively related. Supply depends on the cost of production and the price; however, the law of supply is the relationship between price and quantity. The supply of a commodity depends on many other factors like the state of technology, the productivity of labor, price of related goods, following the rule of ceteris paribus i.e., all other factors remain unchanged.

When the price goes up there is an additional incentive for the producer to supply the goods in the market. This motivates the producer to increase his supply. The cost of production is the minimum price point at which the company can sell without incurring any loss. It is not rational for any producer to accept a price below the cost of production of the product. Anything above the cost price will obviously be the profit. The greater the profit, the greater is the incentive of increasing supply.

2.2 Supply Schedule

The supply schedule of a commodity shows the relationship between its market price and the amount of that commodity that producers are willing to produce and sell, other things held constant[21]. A supply schedule is a tabular representation of various quantities that the supplier will produce and distribute in the market at various price points. Table 2.2 is a hypothetical example of supply from washing powder suppliers in a city market.

---

21. Samuelson, P. A., & Nordhaus, W. D. (2009). Economics 19e.p 5

| Table 2.2 | Supply Schedule of Washing Powder |

Price in USD ($) per pound	Supply of Total no. of packs of 1 pound (in'000) per week
12	150
10	140
8	125
6	110
4	80

Now, when the above supply schedule is represented graphically, the supply curve is obtained as shown in figure 2.2.

| Figure 2.2 | Supply Curve of Washing Powder |

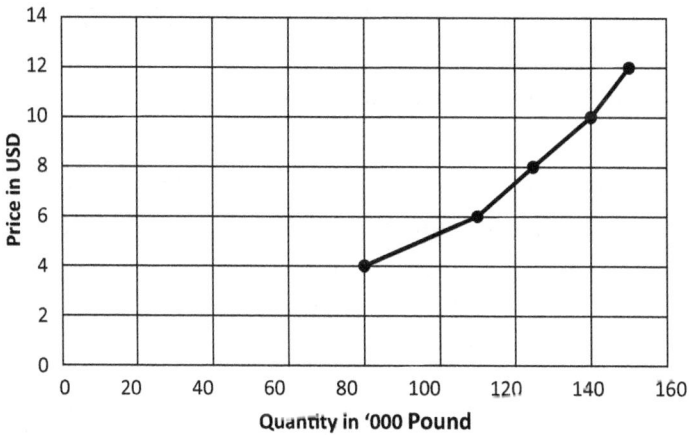

2.3 Equilibrium and Pricing

Till now, we have considered the demand and supply schedules in isolation. Now let's see the situation in a combined table 2.3 that shows both demand and supply together.

| Table 2.3 | Combining Demand and Supply for Washing Powder |

Possible price in $	Demand in '000 pound	Supply in '000 pound	Market position	Pressure on Price
12	100	150	Surplus	Downward
10	110	140	Surplus	Downward
8	125	125	Equilibrium	Neutral
6	150	110	Shortage	Upward
4	180	80	Shortage	Upward

Following Samuelson[22] we note, "A market equilibrium comes at the price at which the quantity demanded equals quantity supplied." This is the price point where market demand and supply meet. The equilibrium price is also called the market-clearing price, as, at this price, all supply and demand orders are fulfilled.

At a price of $12, the customer demanded only 100,000 pounds. This was a lucrative price for the suppliers. So, there was more supply in the market. However, there was excess supply and less demand, which led to more competition among suppliers. Competition forced the suppliers to reduce their prices. This brought down the price, first to $10 and subsequently to $8. At $8, the quantity supplied and the quantity demanded became equal. There was no downward or upward pressure on the price. When

22. Samuelson, P. A., & Nordhaus, W. D. (2009). Economics 19e.p 54

the price continued to decline, the supplier lost interest due to the lesser profitability. Demand soared, but supply was low in the market, leading to a shortage of the product. The condition deteriorated further when the price decreased to the level of $4. The shortage in supply increased further.

In controlled economies, this kind of phenomenon is typically seen. The Government controls and lowers prices to remain popular, leading to shortages of goods in the market. In the erstwhile communist country USSR, there used to be large queues even for basic necessities like bread or shaving cream due to this type of price control.

2.4 Types of Goods

Demand for goods and services is primarily affected by the price, but there are other important determinants too.

The availability and price of complementary and substitute goods often affect the price. Substitute goods are those which can be used in lieu of another. For example, tea drinkers may switch over to coffee. Instead of hamburgers, one may eat hot dogs. Generally, there is a positive relationship between these categories. If the price of hamburgers goes up, the price of hot dogs will also eventually go up.

Complementary goods are those goods that need to be used together; like petrol and cars, or butter and bread. Usually, the prices of complementary goods move in the opposite direction, for example, an increase in the price of petrol may reduce the demand for cars and in effect, their prices.

Consumer incomes are another factor that influences the demand for commodities. Whenever the income of people rises, they have more disposable income on hand and spend a larger amount on goods and services. Now, an income-demand analysis leads to the categorization of various products into four broad groups as such:[23]

i.   Essential consumer goods

ii. Normal goods

iii. Inferior goods

iv. Luxury goods

Essential Consumer goods

Household groceries, food items, electricity, etc. are essential consumer goods which are purchased by all sections in society. The rise in income of consumers initially increases the consumption of essential consumer goods, but then becomes stable.

Normal Goods

Normal goods are goods like electronic gadgets, household furniture, fashionable clothing, etc., the consumption of which goes up with an increase in income. The increase in consumption as income increases varies, depending on the income group of the people. Initially, it increases rapidly, then at a slower rate.

---

23. Dwivedi, D. N. (2016). Microeconomics: Theory and Applications.p.40. Vikas Publishing House.

Inferior goods

Inferior goods are those goods whose consumption decreases with an increase in income. Initially, there may be an increase in the consumption of inferior goods, but eventually, it goes down as soon as the income crosses a certain level. People may opt-out of the public transport system and prefer to travel in their car as soon as their income crosses a certain level. Cheap whiskey may be considered to be an inferior item that people stop consuming as their income increases.

Luxury goods

Luxury goods, often also termed as prestige goods are those categories of goods that people can afford only after reaching a certain level of income. So, an increase in income in the lower classes of society may not have any impact on the demand or prices of luxury goods. Precious stones, luxury cars, jewelry, antiques, etc., fall under this category.

2.5 Shifts in the Demand Curve

Increasing consumer incomes, prices of substitute goods, and government taxes may change the ability and willingness of people to pay for a commodity and therefore alter the demand curve.

When there is a reduction of income tax, it may leave a larger disposable income in the hands of the consumers, and automatically, the demand for goods will go up, shifting the demand curve towards the right. In case the economy is doing well and there is a surge in the wage level, a similar effect is expected to operate on the demand curve. However, when the price of substitute commodities falls, a portion of the demand may shift over to the substitute commodity, pushing the demand curve to the left.

Figure 2.3   Shifts in the Demand Curve

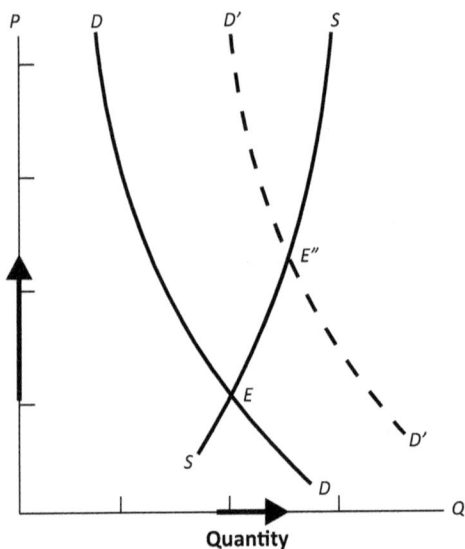

The demand curve may shift due to the following reasons:

a. Changes in consumer income, called the 'income effect'

b. Changes in tastes and preferences of the consumer due to reasons like advertising

c. Substitution effect, wherein the consumer shifts some of his demand over to a substitute product

d. Increase in the price of the complements, which makes the consumer purchase less of the product

A few of the reasons are listed above and the list is not exhaustive, as individual commodity demand may be affected due to various other reasons like entry of new products in the marketplace, competition, obsolescence, change in technology, etc.

2.6 Shifts in the Supply Curve

Figure 2.4 Shifts in the Supply Curve

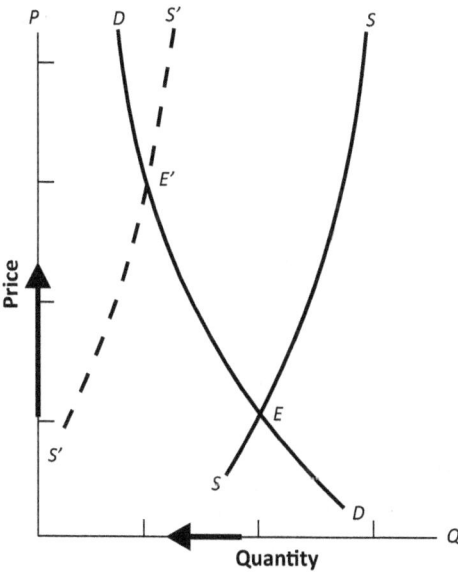

Although price is the main determinant of the quantity supplied of a commodity, there are other factors that affect the quantity of supply. Depending on the increase or decrease in supply at a specific price, the demand curve may shift to the right or to the left. If there is an increase in supply, the supply curve will shift to the right, and vice versa. The supply curve shift may happen due to the following reasons[24]:

a. Changes in technology

Technological upgradation may increase the productivity and total supply of a product. When the textile industry shifts from using ordinary looms to automated looms, there is a massive upscaling of production.

b. Changes in prices of raw materials

Due to a change in the tariff rate, there may be an availability of raw materials and intermediate goods at lower prices. These are inputs for the production process. Cheaper inputs increase the consumption of raw materials, thus increasing the profitability and supply of the product.

c. Prices of substitute products

A production unit may manufacture various types of products. An increase or decrease in one category of the product may make the producer switch production over to the quantity of another line. Suppose, the car manufacturer Ford finds that manufacturing trucks are more profitable. In this case, it may reduce the production of passenger cars, shifting its supply line to the left.

---

24. Samuelson, P. A., & Nordhaus, W. D. (2009). Economics 19e.p 48

d. Government policy

The government's policy of taxation or tariff policies on imported inputs may alter the profitability of a product, and accordingly, the manufacturer may adjust the supply. If the profit margin increases, the manufacturer may like to supply more, shifting the curve towards the right and vice versa.

Discussion Questions

1. Analyze shift in demand and supply curve with increase/ decrease in prices.

2. How can a supply-side constraint create a price rise in the market?

Chapter Summary

◆ Conceptually, demand is a desire for a good backed by the purchasing power and willingness to pay.

◆ The law of demand explains the relationship between the quantity demanded and the price of a commodity.

◆ The law of demand states that all other things remaining constant, the quantity demanded of a commodity increases when the price decreases and decreases when the price increases.

◆ The law of supply states that the supply of a product goes up with an increase in price and goes down with a decrease in its price, other things remaining constant.

◆ Speculative goods and luxury goods are exceptions to the law of demand

◆ A market equilibrium comes at the price at which quantity demanded equals quantity supplied.

◆ Goods are classified into essential consumer goods, normal goods, inferior goods, and luxury goods, depending on their demand curve.

◆ Change in income, tastes, preferences of consumers, and prices of substitute and complementary goods can shift the demand curve.

◆ Changes in technology, prices of raw materials, prices of substitute goods, and government policy can shift the supply curve.

Quiz

1. **All things remaining equal, if the supply increases and demand remains the same, _____.**

   a. the price will fall

   b. the price will remain the same

   c. the price will first increase, then fall

   d. none of the above

2. **All things remaining equal, if the supply decreases and demand remains the same, _____.**

   a. the price will decrease

   b. the price will increase

   c. initially price will increase and then decrease

   d. price will be unaffected

3. **All things remaining equal if the supply remains the same and demand goes up, _____.**

   a. the price will increase

   b. the price will decrease

   c. the price will remain the same

   d. none of the above

4. **All things remaining equal, if the supply remains the same and demand goes down, _____.**

   a. the price will decrease (only for inferior goods)

   b. the price will increase

   c. the price will decrease

   d. the price will decrease only for luxury goods

5. **Price control can lead to _____.**

   a. availability of the product

   b. better quality of life for people

   c. shortage of the product

   d. none of the above

6. **The law of demand is not applicable in the case of _____.**

   a. essential consumer goods

   b. normal goods

   c. consumer durables

   d. speculative goods

7. **The price point is determined at the _____.**

   a. intersection of demand and supply curve

   b. midpoint of demand curve

   c. midpoint of supply curve

   d. depends on the types of goods

8. **The supply curve may shift due to a _____.**

   a. change in technology

   b. change in the price of raw materials

   c. change in government policy

   d. all of the above

9. **Given below are examples of speculative goods, except:**

   a. Company stocks

   b. Gold

   c. Real estate

   d. Coffee

10. **Which of the following is an example of complementary goods?**

    a. Sugar and salt

    b. Wheat and bread

    c. Petrol and car

    d. None of the above

Answers	1 – a	2 – b	3 – a	4 – c	5 – c
	6 – d	7 – a	8 – d	9 – d	10 – c

Chapter 3

Elasticities of Demand and Supply

This chapter introduces the readers to the concept of elasticity and its applications. The concept of price elasticity helps businesses in their pricing decisions. It enables maximizing revenues by keeping the price at an optimum level. Price elasticity is also used in policymaking by the government to maximize revenue by optimizing tariff rates or tax rates. This chapter outlines the measurement of price elasticity of demand and various determinants of price elasticity of demand and supply. We also discuss concepts like cross elasticity and income elasticity of demand.

Key learning objectives of this chapter include the reader's understanding of the following:

- Concepts of price elasticity of demand and supply

- How to calculate price elasticity of demand and supply

- How to calculate arc and point elasticity of demand

- Key determinants of price elasticity of demand and supply
- Concept of cross elasticity of demand
- Concept of income elasticity of demand

3.1 Price Elasticity of Demand

"Elasticity measures the proportionate change in one variable relative to the change in another variable"[25]. There can be various variables like income, price, taxes, etc. A change in income may determine the change in savings. A change in the tax rate may change the quantity purchased by the consumer. Changes in price lead to subsequent changes in the demand and supply of commodities.

"Elasticities provide a quantitative measure of the magnitude of the responsiveness of quantity demanded or supplied to a change in some other variable"[26]. Here, the emphasis is on the measure of the magnitude. The elasticity of demand shows the extent of the change in demand, whereas the law of demand only shows the response of demand to a change in the price. The direction of elasticity is also equally important, as it exhibits whether the variable is directly proportional or inversely proportional.

Samuelson defined price elasticity as follows: "The price elasticity of demand (sometimes simply called price elasticity)

25. Cooper, R., & John, A. A. (2012). Microeconomics: Theory through Applications.

26. Browning, E. K., & Zupan, M. A. (2020). Microeconomics: Theory and applications. John Wiley & Sons.

measures how much the quantity demanded of a good changes when its price changes. The precise definition of price elasticity is the percentage change in quantity demanded divided by the percentage change in price"[27]. Elasticity, therefore, shows the percentage change.

A mathematical definition of price elasticity of demand (Ep) is given below:

Ep= Percentage change in quantity demanded / Percentage change in price

It can be further explained as follows:

$$E_p = -\frac{\Delta Q}{Q_0} \div \frac{\Delta P}{P_0}$$
$$= -\frac{\Delta Q}{Q_0} \times \frac{P_0}{\Delta P}$$
$$= -\frac{\Delta Q}{\Delta P} \times \frac{P_0}{Q_0}$$

Where Q = Original quantity demanded, Po = Original price, Δ Q = change in quantity demanded and Δ P = Change in price.

Let's suppose that a set of beer cans priced at $10 is changed to $12 in a retail store and the corresponding demand also changes from 120 units to 100 units within a day.

In this case, Δ P = $ 10 - $ 12 = - $ 2 and Δ Q = 120 - 100 = 20

$E_p = - (-20/ 2) \times (10/120) = 0.83$

---

27. Samuelson, P. A., & Nordhaus, W. D. (2009). Economics 19e.p 66

3.2 Arc and Point Elasticity

When the price elasticity of demand is measured between two specific points on a demand curve, it is termed as arc elasticity. When the price elasticity is measured at a specific point on the demand curve, it is called point elasticity. Sometimes, the price changes are large and are visible on the demand curve. The price points can be distinguished clearly on the demand curve. On the other hand, in certain cases, the price changes are very small and almost close to zero. When the price changes are high, the movement from one point to another point forming an arc is visible and hence it is called arc elasticity of demand. When the price difference is very small and the difference in price points cannot be distinguished on the demand curve, it is called point elasticity of demand.

| Figure 3.1 | Arc Elasticity of Demand |

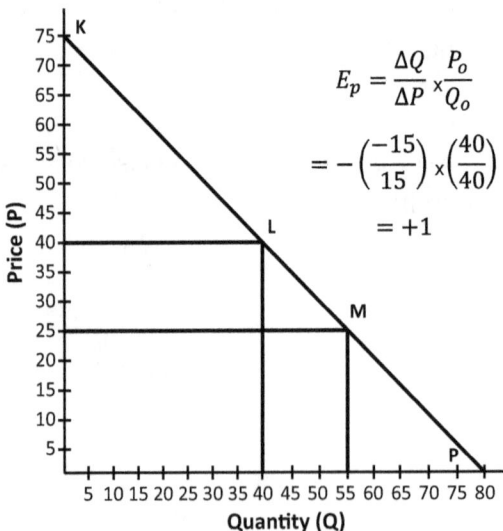

$$E_p = \frac{\Delta Q}{\Delta P} \times \frac{P_o}{Q_o}$$

$$= -\left(\frac{-15}{15}\right) \times \left(\frac{40}{40}\right)$$

$$= +1$$

Here, in the above diagram, the arc elasticity of demand is measured. The original price point was \$40 at point L, which decreased to \$25 at M. The corresponding quantity changed from 40 units to 55 units. So, the original quantity Qo is 40 units, which has now changed to 55 units. The price has decreased by 37.5% (15/40 x 100) and quantity has increased by 37.5% (15/40 x 100). When we calculate the ratio of percentage change in quantity to the percentage change in price, we get 1. The elasticity of demand is 1, as the percentage change in price and quantity are the same.

Arc elasticity of demand should be used with caution as it gives different values for change in direction of price depending on whether price increases or decreases. Instead of a fall in price, if we calculate an increase in price, we will get a different result. So, one needs to be careful during the interpretation of arc elasticity. One remedy to this problem is to consider the average value of the initial and changed quantity or price, rather than taking only the initial value. So, in the first problem, when the price falls to \$25 and quantity increases to 55 units, the calculation can be done as follows:

$$E_p = - (- 15/40{+}55)/(15/40{+}25) = 65/95 = 0.68.$$

Let's assume that in another situation, the price decrease remains the same but the quantity increases to 65 instead of 55. The price elasticity of demand will now be:

$$E_p = - (-25/40{+}65)/(15/40{+}25) = - (-25/105)/(15/65) = 1.03$$

This signifies that a 1 percent change in price will increase the quantity sold by 1.03 percent.

Let's assume a third situation, in which the price drop remains the same, but the quantity sold increases to 90 units. Our price elasticity of demand will now be:

E_p = - (- 50/40+90)/ (15/40+25) = 1.66

Now let's assume that a restaurant is offering a buffet dinner at \$40 and selling 40 plates per night. The F&B manager decides to change the price to \$25, the demand could be 55 packs, 65 plates, and 90 plates, depending on the city. Now revenue is the product of price and quantity and is expressed as:

TR (Total Revenue) = P x Q (Price x Quantity)

We get the following outcomes:

Total Revenue = 40 x 40 = \$1600 in the original situation, say in New York

TR = 25 x 55 = \$1375 when Ep = 0.68 in New York

TR = 25 x 65 = \$1625 when Ep = 1.03 in Beijing

TR = 25 x 90 = \$2250 when Ep = 1.66 in New Delhi

If the restaurant has a revenue-maximizing strategy, the price will be reduced only when E_p >1.

At E_p <1, a decrease in price will decrease the total revenue and at E_p = 1, the revenue will remain unaltered. The restaurant will increase its revenue marginally in Beijing and substantially in New Delhi, but not in New York.

Price elasticity is a key determinant of the pricing strategy in business.

In the case of point elasticity, both Δ Q and Δ P will be close to zero and the elasticity needs to be calculated using the principles of calculus.

Elastic, Inelastic, and Unit Elastic demand

Economists have classified elasticity based on its absolute value. If the elasticity is more than 1, it is termed as elastic, if it is less than 1, it is termed inelastic and in case it equals to 1, it is termed unit elastic.

3.3 Measuring Price Elasticity Using a Demand Function

Price elasticity of demand can also be measured directly using the demand function. Let's consider both a linear and nonlinear demand function.

Let's assume that the linear demand function is given below:

$Q = a - bP$ ------------------------------------- 3.1

At a given price point P1, the demand function will be

$Q_1 = a - bP_1$ ------------------------------3.2

When the price is altered to P2, the demand function becomes

$Q_2 = a - bP_2$ ------------------------------3.3

For measuring the arc elasticity, we need $\Delta Q / \Delta P$ and P/Q

Now, considering equation no 3.2 and 3.3, we can obtain

$\Delta Q / \Delta P = Q_2\text{-}Q_1/ P_2 - P_1 = (a\text{-} bP_2) - (a - bP_1) / P_2 \text{-}P_1 = \text{-} b$

Now, by substituting -b for $\Delta Q / \Delta P$, we find

$E_p = \text{-} b\ P/Q$ --------------------------------------3.4

Now, let us consider a numerical example. Suppose our demand function is as follows:

$Q = 100\ \text{-}10\ P$

By differentiating the demand function, we get,

$\Delta Q / \Delta P = \Delta (100\text{-}10\ P) / \Delta P = \text{-}10$

Now, once we have the value of $\Delta Q / \Delta P$, we can use this for finding out the price elasticity for any price point.

Say, the P = 5, then, Q = 100 – 10 x 5 = 50

Now E_p = -10 x 5/ 50 = -1

Similarly at P = 6, Q = 100- 10 x 6 = 40

Now, E_p = -10 x 6/40 = -2.33

In case of a nonlinear demand function, the multiplicative form will be used:

$Q = aP^{\text{-}b}$

By differentiating both sides, we derive,

$$\frac{\delta Q}{\delta P} = -b\ aP^{-b-1}$$

Now by substituting value of $\dfrac{\delta Q}{\delta P}$ we get,

$$E_P = -b \ aP^{-b-1} x \frac{P}{Q}$$

$$E_P = -b \ \frac{aP^{-b}}{Q}$$

Since $Q = aP^{-b}$

$Ep = -b$

3.4 Determinants of Price Elasticity of Demand

Some commodities have high elasticity, some have a lower elasticity. A higher elasticity means higher responsiveness in demand with a change in price. What determines the absolute value of price elasticity? As per Rittenberg and Tregarthen, "The most important determinants of the price elasticity of demand for a good or service are the availability of substitutes, the importance of the item in household budgets, and time"[28]. We will discuss below the various factors that determine the magnitude of price elasticity of demand.

a. Availability of Substitutes

In case of the availability of close substitutes of a product, the price elasticity will be higher. There is no close substitute for sugar or salt and hence their price elasticity will be lower. But tea can be a substitute for coffee and hence, coffee will be comparatively more elastic. Now, there are numerous varieties of coffee. Colombian coffee can be a close substitute for Brazilian coffee; hence their elasticity will be even more. Often, the same commodity or similar

---

28. Rittenberg, L., & Tregarthen, T. (2013). Principles of Microeconomics: Saylor.p 249.

www.vibrantpublishers.com

commodities are sold under various brand names. Some brands of soap, detergent, or cars are close substitutes for each other. Hence, their elasticity is higher.

The price elasticity of brands is also more than generic products. Suppose Toyota goes for a price rise for their cars. In that case, people have the option of switching over to Honda, Kia, or Ford. There are several options available in each segment. If Nike alone increases their prices, people will switch over to Reebok or Adidas. The availability of a large number of options increases the price elasticity and consumer freedom.

b. Proportion of Income Spent and Importance in the Household Budget

If the proportion of income spent on a commodity is very less and insignificant in the household budget, the demand may be inelastic. A very small portion of our budget is spent on items like baking soda, salt, or pens. Hence, their price increases hardly affect our household budget and we do not pay much attention to the change in their prices. For these items, the price elasticity of demand will be lower. Our household budget is affected by items like clothes, house rent, or the price of gasoline. An increase in the price of denim jeans may make Alice settle for 2 pairs of denim jeans instead of 3. An increase in the house rent may make Peter opt for a residence in a less expensive neighborhood. Michael may start using public transport due to an increase in gasoline prices. These products are found to be more elastic as they affect our household budget.

c. People may take time to respond to price rises.

In the short run, the demand may be price inelastic but over a period of time, the demand may alter. Suppose there is a rise in the newspaper price, only a small number of people will stop reading it the next morning or switch over to another newspaper. So, if we expect a response in a day's time, we will find that the demand for the product is inelastic. But people may switch over to other newspapers or settle for the online edition in the next 3 months. Thus, in the long run, the demand becomes elastic.

d. Nature of commodities

The price elasticity also depends on the nature of goods. Luxury goods may be more elastic than normal goods. Essential goods are expected to be inelastic compared to normal goods. In the case of a price rise, we may buy less fashionable goods or cosmetics but we cannot avoid daily necessities like cereals or electricity. Hence, the latter is more inelastic compared to the former.

e. Proportion of Market Supplied

Dwivedi[29] mentions that "The elasticity of market demand depends also on the proportion of the market supplies at the ruling price. If less than half of the market is supplied, the elasticity of demand will be higher and if more than half of the market is supplied, the elasticity will be lower". If iPhone owners are less in the market; a price drop will generate interest among a large number of buyers as they do not own iPhones due to their high price. A commodity that has a very large market share and a household name

29. Dwivedi, D. N. (2016). Microeconomics: Theory and Applications.p.79. Vikas Publishing House.

like Dell, for example, may not have a similar effect in the case of the laptop or personal computer market.

3.5 Price Elasticity of Supply

The economy has two sides, supply, and demand. When there is a change in the price level, it is not only consumers who react, but businesses too. Manufacturers and suppliers respond to price changes. The responsiveness of the supply side to changes in the price constitutes the price elasticity of supply. Samuelson[30] defined price elasticity of supply as, "The percentage change in quantity supplied divided by the percentage change in price." Dwivedi[31] mentions that "Price elasticity of supply is the measure of the responsiveness of the quantity supplied of a good to the change in its market price". Price elasticity of supply is also defined as "The ratio of the percentage change in quantity supplied of a good or service to the percentage change in its price, all other things remaining unchanged." (Rittenberg & Tregarthen)[32]. All these definitions lead to the magnitude of responsiveness of suppliers to the change in price. It can be expressed mathematically as

30. Samuelson, P. A., & Nordhaus, W. D. (2009). Economics 19e.p 72.

31. Dwivedi, D. N. (2016). Microeconomics: Theory and Applications.p.89. Vikas Publishing House.

32. Rittenberg, L., & Tregarthen, T. (2013). Principles of Microeconomics: Saylor.p 269.

E_p = % Change in quantity supplied / % Change in price

$$= \frac{\frac{\Delta Q}{Q}}{\frac{\Delta P}{P}}$$

$$= \frac{\Delta Q}{\Delta P} \times \frac{P}{Q}$$

The formula for price elasticity of supply is the same as price elasticity of demand, the only exception being the absence of – sign as the supply responds positively to price in contrast to demand.

Suppose the unit export price of garments from Vietnam increases from \$4 to \$5, and the corresponding supply goes up from 8 million pieces to 12 million pieces.

Here $\Delta Q = 4$, $Q = 8$, $\Delta P = 1$, $P = 4$

The price elasticity is calculated as shown below:

$E_p = (4/8)/ (\frac{1}{4}) = 2$

A change in price of 25% increases the supply by 50%.

Supply is called price inelastic when the price elasticity of supply is less than 1; it is unit price elastic if the price elasticity of supply is equal to 1, and it is considered to be price elastic when the price elasticity of supply is greater than 1.

3.6 Determinants of Price Elasticity of Supply

Time is considered to be the most important determinant of price elasticity of supply. In a very short period, the supply of most goods and services is fixed and inelastic. In the long run, it becomes elastic. For creating a new supply, i.e., for the expansion of manufacturing facilities, there is a need for investment, land, and equipment. These factors of production cannot be arranged overnight. If there is an increase in the price of wheat in the international market, it will motivate farmers from Australia to increase their supply to India. However, there is a harvesting period for the new crop. So, supply may only expand after 6 to 9 months. Similarly, maybe Vietnam finds that there is a spurt in the global demand for garments, but to fill the gaps in demand and encash the opportunity, garment manufacturers from Vietnam or Cambodia will take time. The increased production of garments will lead to an increased demand for garment manufacturing machines. There will similarly be a demand for knitting machines and fabric-producing looms. This will create opportunities for the machine manufacturers as well. But they may take even longer to respond to the increasing demand.

The time period may vary depending on the nature of the goods. For perishable items like fast food and dairy products, 1 week may be considered to be a short time. It may be a year for agricultural products. For capital-intensive heavy machinery, it can be even 5 years.

3.7 Cross Elasticity of Demand

The demand for various types of goods is often related. For example, if the price of popcorn is reduced in multiplexes, the demand for movie tickets may go up. Again, when the price of popcorn is reduced, the demand for chips may go down. Popcorn and movies in a multiplex are complementary goods and chips are a substitute for popcorn. The demand for the goods is related to the price of substitutes and complementary goods. Cross price elasticity of demand is the measure used to describe the responsiveness of demand for a good or service to a change in the price of another good or service[33]. This can be shown mathematically as

$E_{a,b}$ = Proportionate change in demand for a/ Proportionate change in the price of b

E a,b is the cross-price elasticity of demand with respect to the price of b.

$$E\ a,b = (\Delta Q_a / Q_a) / (\Delta P_b / P_b)$$

$$= \Delta Q_a \times P_b / \Delta P_b . Q_a$$

Now, let's assume that the price of popcorn decreases from \$3 to \$2 and the sales of chips decrease from 150 packs to 100 packs, then the cross elasticity of demand will be:

$$E_{cp} = 50.\ 3/\ 1 \times 150 = 1$$

Cross elasticity is always positive for substitute goods and it will be negative in the case of complementary goods.

---

33. Rittenberg, L., & Tregarthen, T. (2013). Principles of Microeconomics: Saylor.p 261

In case a price change in one product does not have any impact on the demand of the other, then the products are unrelated and the elasticity will be 0.

By measuring the cross-price elasticity of demand, we may infer the type of goods. The following measures of elasticity will indicate whether the goods or services are complementary, substitute, or unrelated goods.

3.8 Income Elasticity of Demand

When the price of goods or services increases, the purchasing power of people reduces. There is a fall in the real income of the people due to a price rise, which leads to lower demand for goods. This particular phenomenon is covered in a concept called **income elasticity of demand**. The term income elasticity of demand is defined as the percentage change in quantity demanded divided by the percentage change in income, holding other things such as prices constant.

Income elasticity = % change in quantity demanded / % change in income

The income elasticity of demand reflects the shifts in the demand curve at a given level of price. Most of the goods we deal with are normal goods, and in the case of normal goods, the income elasticity of demand is positive. That means when the income rises, the consumption of goods also rises, and when the income reduces, the consumption reduces. We can see this effect in the consumption of wine, seafood, concerts, or a vacation. A rising income allows us to afford a vacation or drink quality wine. Certain types of goods are more affected by income, for example, the purchase of a luxury car or a house, whereas the purchase of essential consumer goods like bread or detergents is less impacted due to changes in price. In case of a rising income, the consumption of inferior goods like public transport or cheaper clothing may fall.

Discussion Questions

1. How does the price elasticity of demand influence the taxation policy in a country?

2. How would you determine price elasticity in case of speculative goods?

Chapter Summary

◆ Elasticity measures the proportionate change in one variable relative to the change in another variable.

◆ Price elasticity is the percentage change in quantity demanded divided by the percentage change in price.

◆ When the price elasticity of demand is measured between two specific points on a demand curve, it is termed arc elasticity.

◆ When the price elasticity is measured at a specific point on the demand curve, it is called point elasticity. Point elasticity is measured only when the change in price is very small and close to zero.

◆ The determinants of price elasticity of demand are the availability of substitutes, the proportion of income spent, the commodity's importance in the household budget, the time period after the price change, the nature of the commodity, and the proportion of market supplied.

◆ Time is considered to be the most important determinant of price elasticity of supply.

◆ Cross price elasticity of demand is the measure used to describe the responsiveness of demand for a good or service to a change in the price of another good or service.

◆ Income elasticity of demand is defined as the percentage change in quantity demanded divided by the percentage change in income, holding other things such as prices constant.

Quiz

1. **Price elasticity is _____ .**

   a. The percentage change in quantity demanded divided by the percentage change in price

   b. The percentage change in price divided by the percentage change in quantity demanded

   c. The percentage change in price divided by the percentage change in supply

   d. None of the above

2. **A cloth merchant will reduce the price of T-shirts when the price elasticity is _____ .**

   a. lesser than 1

   b. more than 1

   c. 1

   d. above 2

3. **If a shopkeeper is selling pencil sets at the rate of $2 and his daily average sales is 50 sets, his average daily revenue is**

   a. $100

   b. $80

   c. $90

   d. $75

4. Ford's pricing team is reviewing the price of F-150 to maximize its revenue out of it, so if the Economic Research Unit informs them that the price elasticity of demand is 1.2, the company will _____. (Assumption: change in price will not affect profit)

   a. increase the price

   b. keep the price unaltered

   c. reduce the price

   d. none of the above

5. The point elasticity of demand is calculated _____.

   a. for normal goods

   b. for luxury goods

   c. for essential consumer goods

   d. when the price change is closer to zero

6. A beauty salon charges $20 for a haircut and its daily revenue is $1600. In case the price elasticity is 1, and the salon decides to drop the price to $10, what will be the new revenue?

   a. $1600

   b. $800

   c. $3200

   d. Cannot be calculated

7. **The income elasticity of demand is _____.**

    a. % Change in quantity demanded / % change in income

    b. % Change in income / % change in quantity demanded

    c. % Change in income / Average demand

    d. None of the above

8. **In case of complementary goods, cross elasticity of demand is**

    _____.

    a. negative

    b. positive

    c. unrelated

    d. positive only in the case of normal goods

9. **In the case of substitute goods, the cross elasticity of demand**

    is _____

    a. negative

    b. positive

    c. unrelated

    d. positive only in the case of normal goods

10. Following is the main determinant of price elasticity of supply:

a. Government policy

b. Technology

c. Consumer demand

d. Time

Answers	1 – a	2 – b	3 – a	4 – c	5 – d
	6 – a	7 – a	8 – a	9 – b	10 – d

This page is intentionally left blank

Chapter 4

Consumer Behavior - Cardinal Utility Approach

This chapter introduces the reader to the theory of consumer behavior. Consumer behavior tries to answer the question of how a consumer responds to market conditions like changes in price. This chapter outlines the concept of utility and whether the utility is measurable or cardinal. The chapter discusses the concept of marginal utility, total utility, and the law of diminishing marginal utility in detail. The purpose of this chapter is to explain consumer behavior theories to the readers so that they can appreciate and understand how buyers make a purchase decision in a supermarket or in a grocery store when they have a limited budget for their needs.

Key learning objectives include the reader's understanding of the following:

- Theories and applications of consumer behavior
- Concept of utility and its measurement

- How to measure total utility

- How to derive marginal utility

- The law of diminishing marginal utility

- How a consumer can maximize his or her utility

- Consumers' equilibrium

- Limitations of cardinal utility approach

4.1 Concept of Cardinal Utility

Economists have assumed that consumers try to maximize their utility. But what is utility? Samuelson and Nordhaus mention that "In explaining consumer behavior, economics relies on the fundamental premise that people choose those goods and services they value most highly"[34]. For example, Peter is feeling hungry and has $5 with him. He has the option of buying a coke and a burger with this money. He also would love to have a beer. But as he is hungry, a burger will give him more satisfaction than a can of beer. Thus, the satisfaction obtained out of a good or service is termed as its utility. For Peter, the utility of a burger is more than that of a beer. Samuelson defines utility as *satisfaction*. Now, the question arises: can utility be measured? Classical and neoclassical economists believed that utility could be measured with numbers or in terms of weight, height, or temperature. Modern economists like Vilfredo Pareto, W.E. Johnson, A.L. Bowley, and John R. Hicks believe that it could not be measured in numbers but could be classified in ordinal terms like *more than*

---

34. Samuelson, P. A., & Nordhaus, W. D. (2009). Economics 19e.p 84.

or less than[35]. Thus, consumer behavior has two approaches: the Cardinal Utility Approach and the Ordinal Utility Approach. In this chapter, our focus is on the Cardinal Utility, and in the next chapter, we will discuss Ordinal Utility.

Walrus, a neoclassical economist, introduced the term 'util' meaning a 'unit of utility.' He used money as the measure of utility with the assumption that the utility of a good is equal to the amount of money the consumer is ready to spend on it and 1 util = 1 currency. Furthermore, the marginal utility (explained later in the chapter) of money is also assumed to be constant[36].

This theory indicates that if Peter was ready to spend $5 on a can of coke and a burger, his utility = 5 utils. If he wants to spend the same amount on buying a set of stationery, the utility will be the same, i.e. 5 utils.

4.2 Total and Marginal Utility

Utility is the derived satisfaction. Now, this is dependent on the quantity of money spent. When Peter spent $5, he obtained 5 'utils' of utility. When he spends more, his utility will go up. However, utility is not exactly proportional to the amount of money spent. By spending $500, Peter may not get 500 utilities. Does this sound confusing? We will try to understand this with the concept of *marginal utility of demand.*

---

35. Dwivedi, D. N. (2016). Microeconomics: Theory and Applications.p.119. Vikas Publishing House.

36. Dwivedi, D. N. (2016). Microeconomics: Theory and Applications.p.108. Vikas Publishing House.

Mary is hungry. She buys a sandwich for $2. She feels like having one more and goes for the second one. Now Mary is almost full. But she has a travel plan lined up. It may be a long time before she finds a food joint. She decides to buy the third sandwich. Are the utilities the same for the first, second, and third sandwiches? Of course not! If the food joint allows her a 25 percent discount on the fourth sandwich but a take-away is not permitted, Mary may refuse to buy further sandwiches even at a discount. The maximum utility derived by Mary was when she ate the first sandwich and subsequently her utility was reduced.

Now if we assign U_1, U_2, U_3, and U_4 utility to the first, second, third and the fourth sandwich, the total utility,

$$TU = U_1 + U_2 + U_3 + U_4 \text{ --- (4.1)}$$

In case there are n no of units consumed, then equation 4.1 can be written as

$$TU_n = U_1 + U_2 + U_3 + U_4 + \text{.................... } U_n \text{ ----------------(4.2)}$$

Marginal utility is the change in total utility due to the consumption of the additional unit.

Marginal Utility $MU_n = TU_n - TU_n\text{-}1$ ------------------------- (4.3)

We can also write $MU = \Delta TU / \Delta C$

Here ΔTU is the change in the total utility and ΔC is the change in consumption by 1 unit.[37]

---

37. Dwivedi, D. N. (2016). Microeconomics: Theory and Applications.p.109. Vikas Publishing House.

4.3 Law of Diminishing Marginal Utility

| Table 4.1 | **Marginal and Total Utility** |

Units of Sandwich	Total Utility	Marginal Utility-Formula	Marginal Utility
1	8	TU_1	8
2	14	$TU_2 - TU_1$	6
3	18	$TU_3 - TU_2$	4
4	20	$TU_4 - TU_3$	2
5	20	$TU_5 - TU_4$	0
6	18	$TU_6 - TU_5$	-2

In the above table, the consumption of sandwiches by Mary is represented. We can see that the marginal utility goes down with an increase in the consumption of sandwiches. The total utility obtained by Mary went up but the marginal utility went down. Following the definition of Salvatore[38], we find that "Marginal utility (MU) is the extra utility received from consuming one additional unit of the good per unit of time while holding constant the quantity consumed of all other commodities". Here, the relevance of time is to be noted minutely. A purchase for future consumption cannot be considered under the law of diminishing marginal utility. The consumption of all other commodities is also assumed to be held constant.

"The amount by which total utility rises with the consumption of an additional unit of a good, service, or activity, all other things remaining unchanged, is marginal utility"[39]. This definition

---

38. Salvatore, Dominick, 2008. "Microeconomics: Theory and Applications," OUP Catalogue, Oxford University Press, edition 5. Chapter 3. Page no 57

39. Rittenberg, L., & Tregarthen, T. (2013). Principles of Microeconomics: Saylor.p 356.

includes all kinds of goods and services or even activities while keeping other things unchanged, be it consumption of other goods or units of time. So, the example can be extended from sandwiches to an event. We may not have the same utility when we visit the same opera for the second time.

Marginal utility theory holds good under the assumption that the consumer is rational, his or her tastes and preferences remain unchanged, and there is no break in consumption. A break in consumption can bring his appetite back and the utility may change once more.

An exception to this is seen in the event of accumulation of money or collection of hobby items like stamps and coins of various countries, antique pieces, or collection of books[40].

Figure 4.1   Total and Marginal Utility

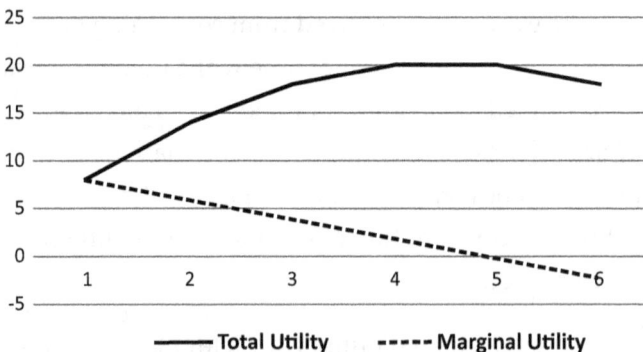

40. Dwivedi, D. N. (2016). Microeconomics: Theory and Applications.p.111. Vikas Publishing House

The above diagram is a graphical illustration of the hypothetical example of sandwiches consumed by Mary. The total utility of Mary had been increasing till the fourth sandwich, then it was zero for the fifth sandwich. With a further intake, her total utility decreased further. Consumption of food beyond a point can make one uncomfortable. The marginal utility for Mary was diminishing continuously with the increasing intake of sandwiches. In the above graph, we can see that total utility had been initially increasing, then it slowed down and finally declined, while the marginal utility is diminishing with an increase in quantity intake.

The law of diminishing marginal utility can also explain the negative slope of a demand curve. With a decrease in price, a consumer is willing to buy a larger quantity of a commodity. If a consumer is buying a dozen apples at $8, he may buy more only when the price drops down to $5. At the price of $8, he will not buy more as the purchase of the next unit has lesser utility for him. He will buy more only when the price is reduced to match his diminished marginal utility. This explains why as per the law of demand, people buy increased quantities when the price drops.

4.4 Consumers' Equilibrium

The cardinal utility approach is based on the following assumptions[41]:

a. Rationality of the Consumer

In the case of the cardinal utility approach, it is assumed that consumers are rational. They know their own requirements well. Their choices are determined by the utility of the goods. He buys goods that have the highest utility for them..

b. Limited Income of the Consumer

Consumers have a limited income. They have a budget constraint and need to fit their requirements, needs, and wishes within their budgets.

c. Maximization of Satisfaction

As rational beings, consumers try to maximize their satisfaction within their limited incomes.

d. Utility Can Be Quantified

Utility can be measured and can be quantified. It is measurable in cardinal numbers.

e. Utility of Money is Constant

Irrespective of the monetary status of the person, the utility of money remains the same. It is constant and equal for rich and poor alike.

---

41. Dwivedi, D. N. (2016). Microeconomics: Theory and Applications.p.111. Vikas Publishing House

f. Additive Property of Utility

Utility is not only measurable with numbers; it can also be added to determine the total utility. For example, if Alice consumes an apple and an orange with 2 and 3 utils of utility respectively, her total utility out of the consumption of these two fruits (1 apple and 1 orange) is 5 utils.

Consumers reach the equilibrium position and maximize their total utility at a particular price within their limited resources. Resources mean the budget or money consumers have for maximizing their utility. The question is how the consumer reaches this equilibrium point by allocating the budget among various goods and services.

Principle of Equi-Marginal Utility

Cardinal utility analysis is based on the law of equi- marginal utility. Consumer Equilibrium is also explained through this principle. In this concept, it is assumed that the consumer is rational and he tries to maximize his utility within his budget by substituting various goods according to their utility. A consumer can substitute an orange for an apple. Now the important points to consider are the marginal utility of goods and their prices. The law of equi-marginal utility states that "A consumer will achieve maximum satisfaction or utility when the marginal utility of the last dollar spent on a good is exactly the same as the marginal utility of the last dollar spent on any other good"[42]. This means that the marginal utility of money spent on each good is equal at the equilibrium point.

---

42. Samuelson, P. A., & Nordhaus, W. D. (2009). Economics 19e.p 87.

Suppose, the marginal utility of money is MU_m.

Now, the marginal utility of money spent on a good is equal to the marginal utility of the goods divided by the price of the goods[43].

Now, suppose the consumer buys two goods, X and Y.

As per the law of equi-marginal utility,

$$MU_m = MU_X / P_X = MU_Y / P_Y$$

Where, MU_X is the marginal utility of good X, P_X is the price of good X.

MU_Y is the marginal utility of good Y and P_Y is the price of the good Y.

Now, if $MU_X / P_X > MU_Y / P_Y$, then the consumer will continue substituting X for Y till both become equal.

Now $MU_X / P_X = MU_Y / P_Y$ can happen at various levels of expenditure. But consumer equilibrium will be only achieved when the marginal utility of money spent on each good becomes equal to the marginal utility of the money it costs, i.e.,

$$MU_m = MU_X / P_X = MU_Y / P_Y$$

In a normal circumstance, the number of goods and services consumed will be much more than two goods and the above equation will hold good for any number of items, i.e.,

$$MU_X / P_X = MU_Y / P_Y = \ldots\ldots\ldots\ldots = MU_N / P_N = MU_m$$

---

43. Ahuja, H. L. (2019). Advanced Economic Theory: Microeconomic Analysis.p.122 S. Chand Publishing

4.5 Drawbacks of the Cardinal Utility Approach

The cardinal utility approach is not accepted by modern economists as the fundamental assumption that utility can be quantified objectively is rejected. Utility is a subjective concept and cannot be measured objectively. It is based on our perception and human psychology. The attempt to quantify utility is useful but cannot be verified empirically[44].

Secondly, in the case of the cardinal utility approach, the marginal utility of money is considered to be constant. However, like all other goods and services, the marginal utility of money also changes. The marginal utility of a $10 bill is not the same when you have $1000 or $20 with you.

Thirdly, the cardinal utility approach holds under the condition of ceteris paribus. However, all conditions do not remain the same during consumption. The income of the people and substitution of the goods play a role in influencing the utility of the goods.

Finally, the measurement of the marginal utility of demand with the cardinal approach is hypothetical and perception-driven. The law is accepted as an axiom without empirical evidence[45].

---

44. Schroeder, C., & Yitzhaki, S. (2017). Revisiting the evidence for cardinal treatment of ordinal variables. European Economic Review, 92, 337-358.

45. Dwivedi, D. N. (2016). Microeconomics: Theory and Applications.p.115. Vikas Publishing House

Discussion Questions

1. Does marginal utility of demand influence family budget? Answer with examples of all kinds of goods like normal, essential consumer goods etc. consumed by a family.

2. Analyze a situation in which Peter consumes multiple sandwiches at an outlet at the same price. How does his utility change during the meal?

Chapter Summary

♦ The satisfaction obtained out of a good or service is termed as utility.

♦ Consumers try to maximize their utility.

♦ Classical and neoclassical economists believed that utility could be measured with numbers.

♦ Modern economists believed that utility could not be measured in numbers but could be classified in ordinal terms like more than or less than.

♦ In the cardinal approach utility is measured with a unit known as 'util'.

♦ Marginal utility is the additional utility obtained through the consumption of an extra unit of a good or a service when all other things remain unchanged

♦ In the cardinal utility approach, it is assumed that the marginal utility of money is constant

♦ The law of diminishing marginal utility is accepted as an axiom without empirical evidence

Quiz

1. Choose the correct statement.

    a. Utility can be measured numerically in the cardinal approach

    b. Utility can be measured numerically in the ordinal approach

    c. Utility can be measured through the law of equi-marginal utility of demand

    d. None of the above

2. Choose the correct statement.

    a. Utility remains constant throughout our consumption

    b. Utility cannot be determined as it is a vague term

    c. Utility diminishes with an increase in consumption

    d. Utility increases with an increase in consumption

3. Choose the correct statement.

    a. Util is the unit of utility

    b. Marginal utility diminishes when we collect hobby items like stamps

    c. The total utility curve is a straight line

    d. The marginal utility of the second can of coke is more than 1st can

4. **When we buy groceries for a week, the marginal utilities of the items do not decrease because**

   a. It is not applicable for household consumption

   b. Groceries are normal goods

   c. Groceries are essential consumer goods

   d. The unit of time changes

5. **Modern economists believe that:**

   a. Utility cannot be determined

   b. Utility cannot be expressed in quantity but can be compared

   c. Utility can be expressed numerically

   d. None of the above

6. **The law of equi-marginal utility states that _____.**

   a. utility derived from the last dollar is equal for all goods

   b. all goods consumed by a rational consumer have the same utility

   c. the marginal utility of money will be equal to the utility derived from the last dollar

   d. options a and c

7. **The cardinal utility approach assumes that the _____.**

    a. utility of money changes

    b. marginal utility of money is constant

    c. utility of money cannot be measured

    d. utility of money depends on the amount of money held

8. **Theory of Marginal utility of money is only applicable**

    _____.

    a. when the consumption of all other goods remains constant

    b. when the marginal utility of money is constant

    c. when it is calculated per unit of time

    d. all of the above

9. **Melinda had a third serving during lunch and felt**
    uncomfortable, she had a _____.

    a. negative marginal utility

    b. zero marginal utility

    c. cannot be said

    d. marginal utility cannot be negative

10. **Jack bought a book by Agatha Christie. He liked it so much that he bought another one. He got engrossed in the book and ordered a third one.**

a. The marginal utility of the third book will be the least

b. The purchase here does not follow the law of diminishing marginal utility

c. The purchases do not have utility

d. None of the above

Answers	1 – a	2 – c	3 – a	4 – d	5 – b
	6 – d	7 – b	8 – d	9 – a	10 – b

This page is intentionally left blank

Chapter 5

Consumer Behavior – Ordinal Utility Approach

This chapter will help readers understand consumer behavior using the ordinal utility approach. From the previous chapter, we know that the cardinal utility approach was adopted by classical and neoclassical economists like Jeremy Bentham, Gossen, Jevons, Alfred Marshall, etc., while, modern economists like Vilfredo Pareto, Slutsky, Johnson, and Bowley[46] followed the ordinal utility approach, which measures utility subjectively and relatively without assigning any number. We can state whether the utility of an umbrella is more or less for a particular consumer than a raincoat on a rainy day, but we cannot assign numbers to measure their relative utilities. This chapter outlines the concept of ordinal utility and explains the concepts of indifference curves and their properties. The chapter also explains the budgetary constraints of a consumer and how the budget line

---

46. Dwivedi, D. N. (2016). Microeconomics: Theory and Applications.p.119. Vikas Publishing House

is graphically represented. Lastly, it discusses the advantages and criticisms of the indifference curve approach.

Key learning objectives of this chapter include the reader's understanding of the following:

- Concept of ordinal utility

- Definition of indifference curve

- How to graphically represent indifference curves

- Various properties of indifference curves

- Concepts of budgetary constraints and budget line

- How to graphically represent the budget constraints and budget line

- Advantages of the indifference curve approach

- Criticisms of the indifference curve approach

5.1 Concept of Ordinal Utility

In our day-to-day life, we need to make choices. We need to decide whether we will renovate our house or go for a vacation, or whether to buy a new car or invest the money in a pension fund. Should I opt for a pizza for lunch or settle for a leafy salad? There are numerous choices that consumers have to make. Consumers are assumed to be rational and are therefore supposed to choose the item that gives them the most utility. They will not settle for something that has a comparatively lower utility. Ordinal utility does not attach any number or quantitative measure while measuring utility, rather it is an expression indicating a consumer's preference. It explains whether a consumer likes a good more or less compared to another good. Modern economists reject the notion of cardinal utility, and hence, the theory of demand is based on ordinal utility. Samuelson and Nordhaus mention that, "Ordinal variables are ones that we can rank in order, but for which there is no measure of the quantitative difference between the situations"[47]. Salvatore[48] mentions that "Ordinal utility only ranks the utility received from consuming various amounts of a good or a basket of goods". In the discussion of ordinal utility, numbers can be attached as per the preference of the customers. However, the absolute values of these numbers carry no meaning. Suppose, we say that Mary had obtained 10 utils out of a sandwich and 20 utils out of a hamburger, it does not mean that she got double the utility by consuming a hamburger. It only shows that a hamburger has more utility for her than a sandwich. Similarly, if we assign numbers like 4, 6, 8, 10, and 12 respectively for a sandwich, burger, hot dog, pizza, and a wrap, it just helps us in ranking the ordinal utilities; the numbers do not indicate the weightage they have according to the consumer's preferences.

"The ideas of Jevons and his co-workers led directly to the modern theories of ordinal utility and indifference curves developed by Vilfredo Pareto, John Hicks, R.G.D. Allen, Paul Samuelson, and others, in which the Benthamite ideas of measurable cardinal utility are no longer needed"[49]. Today, the concept of the ordinal utility approach lies at the forefront in the discourse of consumer decision-making. In the next section,

---

47. Samuelson, P. A., & Nordhaus, W. D. (2009). Economics 19e.p 89.

48. Salvatore, Dominick, 2008. "**Microeconomics: Theory and Applications**," OUP Catalogue, Oxford University Press, edition 5. Chapter 3. Page no 60

49. Samuelson, P. A., & Nordhaus, W. D. (2009). Economics 19e.p 87.

we will focus on the concept of indifference curves based on the ordinal utility theory.

5.2 Indifference Curve

Indifference curves are an alternative approach to explaining consumer behavior and buyer choices. It is considered to be an advanced approach to understanding consumer utility.

A consumer may have a set of bundles for consumption. Let's take the example of a combination of apples and bananas for the consumer's consumption. He may substitute apples for bananas or bananas for apples. However, each combination is supposed to give him equal utility. As far as satisfaction or utility is concerned, he will be indifferent between various combinations. In table no 5.1, various combinations of apples and bananas consumed by this consumer, Peter is shown. Now, it is clear that for getting an additional apple, the consumer has to forego some quantities of bananas. This enables the consumer to have his utility constant throughout the indifference curve. All the points on the indifference curve will give the consumer the same satisfaction. The consumer remains on the same indifference curve without any change in his utility, and the curve slopes downward. The rate at which the consumer can substitute bananas for apples is called the **Marginal Rate of Substitution (MRS).**

Table 5.1

Combination	Quantity of Apples	Quantity of Bananas	MRS
A	1	20	-
B	2	10	10:1
C	3	5	5:1
D	4	3	2:1
E	5	2	1:1

In table 5.1, we can notice that initially, the consumer substituted 10 bananas for 1 apple. With an increase in the stock of apples, the utility of apples drops and in the next round of consumption, he substituted only 5 bananas for 1 apple. This trend of falling utility of the apples with the increase in consumption of apples is precisely **the Law of Diminishing Marginal Rate of Substitution (MRS).** We can further see that with an increase in the stock of apples, the consumer further exchanges only 2 bananas for 1 apple, and then, the utility becomes the same for both apples and bananas, with the Marginal Rate of Substitution being 1:1. Due to the law of diminishing marginal rate of substitution, the indifference curve slopes downward and its shape is convex to the origin.

| Figure 5.1 | Indifference Curve |

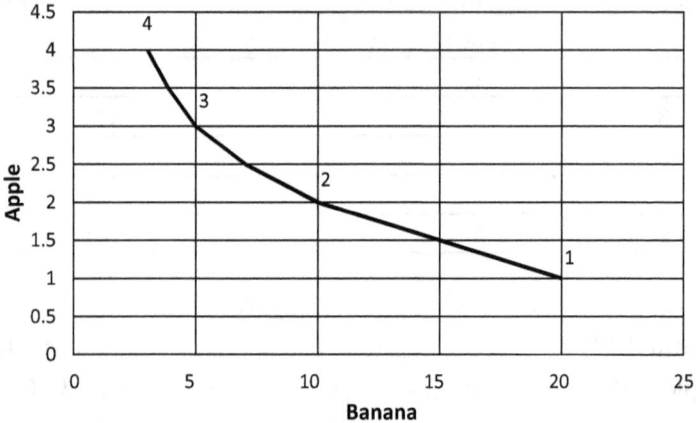

In case the two commodities are perfect substitutes for each other, like currency notes and coins, the MRS will be constant and it will not diminish. For a consumer, it does not matter whether he uses coins or notes as the value is the same. In the international forex market, the foreign exchange dealer will be ready to exchange Euros for US Dollars at the prevailing rate of exchange or vice versa. For the dealer, the valuation matters, not the currency. The dollar is a perfect substitute for the Euro. In these cases, the indifference curves will be straight lines. But in general, for consumption items, there is a diminishing marginal utility, and the indifference curve slopes downward, its shape convex in nature.

Now, let's assume that the consumer has a bundle of goods, x, and y, and there are sets of bundles like (x_1, y_1), (x_2, y_2), and (x_3, y_3). Now, a consumer will prefer (x_2, y_2) more than (x_1, y_1) only when the former combination has at least one good extra and no goods lesser than the latter. This is called the **monotonic preference** of the consumer.

Indifference Map

When we graphically present a set of indifference curves showing various levels of consumers' utility, it is called an indifference map (See figure 5.2). A particular indifference curve, IC_1 or IC_2 has all the points on it with the same utilities. However, there is a difference in utility between the points on two separate indifference curves, IC_1 and IC_2. Consumer utility is higher when placed on a higher indifference curve and vice versa.

In figure 5.2, the indifference curve IC_3 has the highest utility followed by IC_2, and IC_1 has the least utility.

Figure 5.2	Indifference Map

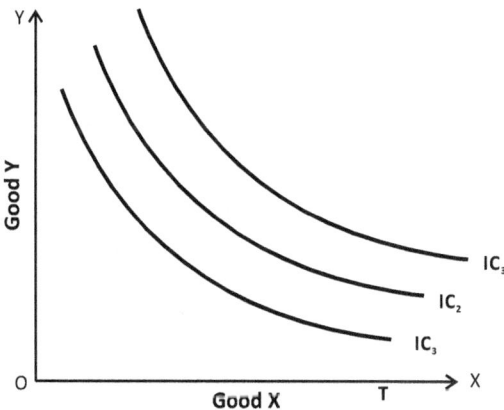

Following Rittenberg & Tregarthen, we find that, "Each indifference curve suggests combinations among which the consumer is indifferent. Curves that are higher and to the right are preferred to those that are lower and to the left"[50].

50.Rittenberg, L., & Tregarthen, T. (2013). Principles of Microeconomics: Saylor.p 390.

5.3 Properties of Indifference Curves

Indifference curves are usually negatively sloped, cannot intersect and are convex to the origin[51]. The unique properties of indifference curves are discussed below.

a. **Indifference curves have a negative slope.**

The negative slope of indifference curves indicates that the goods are substitutes for each other. Apples are a substitute for bananas, so when the consumption of apples increases, the consumption of bananas goes down. When we compare two baskets of goods with the same level of satisfaction, if there is a lesser quantity of one good in one basket, then there has to be a larger quantity in the other.

If the indifference curve had a positive slope, it would mean that a lower amount of goods gives the same level of satisfaction as a larger amount of goods. In figure 5.2, at position B, both the quantities x and y are more compared to position A. This is an impossible situation in an indifference curve, as satisfaction across the same indifference curve remains the same. Hence, by definition, indifference curves need to have a negative slope.

b. **Indifference curves do not intersect each other.**

By definition, various points in an indifference curve provide equal satisfaction or utility. Now, let's consider a situation as shown in figure 5.2, where two curves are intersecting each other. The curves show three different points A, B, and C with three different amounts of the

---

51. Salvatore, Dominick, 2008. "Microeconomics: Theory and Applications," OUP Catalogue, Oxford University Press, edition 5. Chapter 3. Page no 64

quantity of x and y. So, the satisfaction cannot be the same at all three points. If an indifference intersects another one at a point (C in figure 5.2), then equal utility is obtained at the point of intersection but, there are higher and lower utilities across the same indifference curve which flouts the very definition of indifference curve.

Figure 5.3 **Positive slope curve and interesting curves (cannot be indifference curves)**

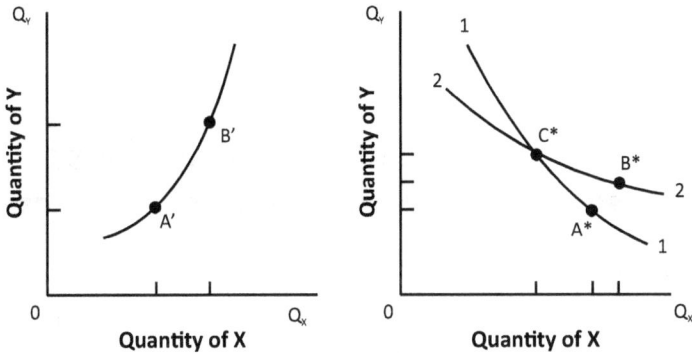

c. **Indifference curves have a convex shape.**

As there is a diminishing marginal rate of substitution for normal goods, the indifference curves are convex to the origin. The convexity of indifference curves implies that the marginal rate of substitution between two goods decreases as the consumer alters his purchase points along the indifference curve. Furthermore, the goods are not perfect substitutes for each other. In case they are perfect substitutes like currency notes and coins, the indifference curves may be straight lines. But most of the goods are imperfect substitutes for each other and hence, the indifference curve is convex in nature.

d. Indifference curves on a higher level contain more utility.

The indifference curve on the higher right-side plane represents a greater amount of both goods. If you refer to figure 5.2, you will find that IC_3 has more quantities of both x and y compared to IC_2. Again, IC_2 has a greater combination of x and y compared to IC_1. Consuming more quantities of goods leads to greater satisfaction or utility and therefore, the indifference curves on the right on a higher plane have more utility.

5.4 Budgetary Constraints and Budget Lines

In the words of Salvatore: "In economics jargon, we say that the consumer faces a *budget constraint* due to his or her limited income and the given prices of goods"[52]. Consumers' incomes are limited and they need to fulfill their needs with their limited resources. Let's look at an example where a consumer has allocated a monthly budget of $100 per month towards fruits. Now, the amount of bananas and kiwis consumed by him has to be within the budget. Let's assume that a Kiwi costs $4 and a banana costs $1. The consumer has the liberty to purchase a total of 25 kiwis or 100 bananas separately. He can also buy 10 kiwis and 60 bananas with his budget or he can go for various combinations like 15 kiwis and 40 bananas or 20 kiwis and 20 bananas. The consumer may decide not to exhaust his entire

---

52. Salvatore, Dominick, 2008. **"Microeconomics: Theory and Applications**," OUP Catalogue, Oxford University Press, edition 5. Chapter 3. Page no 71

budget and may instead choose to settle for less. He may choose to buy 18 kiwis and 18 bananas or 15 pieces of each fruit. Lower consumption will not hurt his budget. But he cannot afford to go for 50 bananas and 20 kiwis as it will cost him more than $100. This is the **budget constraint** faced by the consumer. Dwivedi[53] mentions, "The limitedness of income acts as a constraint on the utility-maximizing behavior of the consumer. This is known as a budgetary constraint".

Let's assume that the prices of goods x and y are denoted as Px and Py while the quality of consumption is Qx and Qy respectively, and M is the money income of the consumer. Now, assuming that the consumer spends his entire income on the two commodities, x, and y, we may write,

$$M = P_x . / Q_x + P_y / Q_y \text{--(5.1)}$$

Following equation 5.1, we can write,

$$Q_x = (M - P_y \times Q_y) / P_x \text{--------------------------------------(5.2)}$$

$$Q_y = (M – P_x \times Q_x) / P_y \text{--------------------------------------(5.3)}$$

Now, if we consider $Q_y = 0$ in equation 5.2 and $Q_x = 0$ in equation 5.3, we find that:

$$Q_x = M/ P_x \text{ and } Q_y = M/ P_y$$

When we plot a line with (Q_x, 0) and (Q_y, 0), we get a negatively-sloped straight line. On the Y-axis, the value of Q_y is plotted and on the X-axis, the value of Q_x is plotted. This is the price line or budget line.

53. Dwivedi, D. N. (2016). *Microeconomics: Theory and Applications*.p.127. Vikas Publishing House

The budget line can shift due to a change in consumers' income and the price of the commodities. The increase in income will shift the budget line to the right with the same slope if the price of goods is unaltered. The slope of the line will change with a change in the price of the commodities.

Figure 5.4   Budget Line

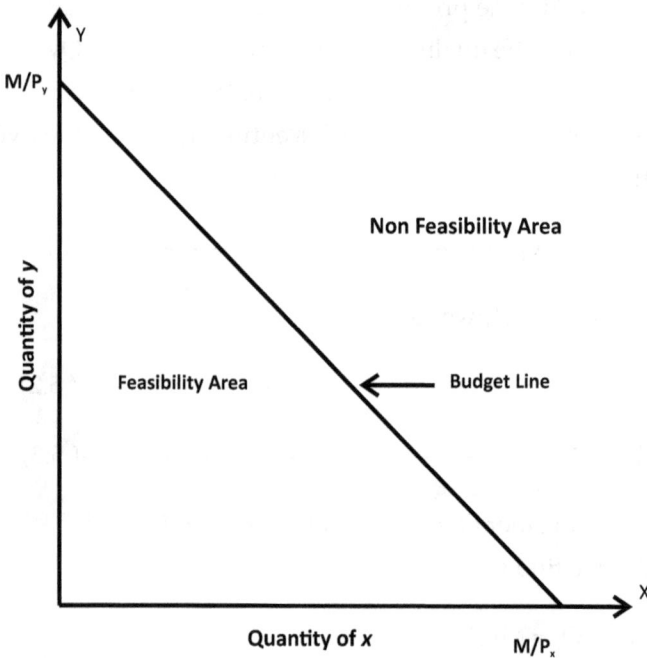

5.5 Advantages and Criticisms of the Indifference Curve Approach

Advantages of the Indifference Curve Approach

The ordinal utility and indifference curve approach are conceptually superior and has helped in the advancement of the consumer behavior theory[54].

a. It does not assume a constant utility of money. It is more realistic as it does not attach any quantitative measure to utility which is difficult to justify.

b. The goods can be classified into substitutes and complementary goods based on the shape of the curve.

c. The indifference curve approach can show the consumer's surplus and is therefore considered to be a great tool for welfare economics. This helps governments in policy formulation.

Criticism of the Indifference Curve Approach

a. It is based on an axiom. The theory does not establish the convex shape of the indifference curve.

b. It assumes that the consumer has perfect knowledge about his choices and that those choices are rational. This assumption is not always correct. Consumer preferences keep shifting. Consumers are not always able to order their preferences. Their preferences depend on factors like income, availability, price, tastes, etc.

---

54. Stoyanov, V. (2018). Comparative Analysis between Cardinal Utility and Ordinal Utility. Ikonomicheski i Sotsialni Alternativi, (4), 133-144.

c. The indifference curve approach does not consider the
    influence of marketing activities and advertising on
    consumer preferences. Often, consumer preferences change,
    like sudden impulse purchases and immediate urges.
    The tenet of consumer rationality is often challenged by
    behavioral economists.

d. The indifference curve can be graphically represented when
    the combination of quantities consumed is made out of the
    two goods. In reality, a consumer buys several goods and
    services. Representing the combination of multiple such
    items needs higher computational skills and mathematical
    tools. The indifference curve may not be fully able to explain
    this kind of complex scenario.

After studying both cardinal and ordinal utility, we may
conclude that despite a few limitations, the ordinal utility theory
is an improvement over the cardinal utility approach. The ordinal
utility theory and indifference curve approach can help us in
understanding consumer welfare and aid the government in
policymaking.

Discussion Questions

1. Analyze the properties of an indifference curve and explain how the utility remains same at all points of the curve.

2. Compare the cardinal and ordinal utility theory and explain which one you find to be more effective for economic analysis.

Chapter Summary

◆ Ordinal utility does not attach any number or quantitative measure to utility, rather it is an expression indicating a consumer's preferences.

◆ Ordinal utility ranks consumer preferences for various combinations of two goods or services.

◆ The consumer is indifferent between various combinations of goods on the points of an indifference curve and derives the same utility.

◆ The Law of Diminishing Marginal Rate of Substitution shows that the marginal rate of substitution (MRS) declines as a consumer consumes more and more of a product.

◆ Due to the Law of Diminishing Marginal Rate of Substitution, the indifference curve slopes downward and its shape is convex to the origin.

◆ In case the two commodities are perfect substitutes for each other, the MRS will be constant and it will not diminish.

◆ When a set of indifference curves showing various levels of consumer's utility is presented graphically, it is called an indifference map.

◆ Consumer utility is higher on a higher indifference curve compared to other lower indifference curves and vice versa.

◆ Any point beyond the budget line on the indifference curve is not feasible.

Quiz

1. **The concept of Ordinal utility allows:**

   a. To measure the utility in absolute numbers

   b. Compare utility as less than or more than

   c. It can be both a and b

   d. None of the above

2. **On an indifference curve, the marginal rate of substitution _____.**

   a. increases

   b. remains constant

   c. decreases

   d. cannot be said

3. **In case the two products are perfect substitutes for each other, then the MRS will be _____.**

   a. constant

   b. decreasing

   c. increasing

   d. cannot be said

4. **In case the two products are perfect substitutes for each other then the shape of the indifference curve will be _____.**

    a. convex to the origin

    b. concave to the origin

    c. not a curve, it will be a straight line

    d. none of the above

5. **A consumer buys apples and bananas in the following combinations (5,2) (6,1) (7, 3). Which combinations can form an indifference curve?**

    a. (5,2) and (6,1)

    b. (5,2) and (7,3)

    c. (6,1) and (7,3)

    d. None of them

6. **In an indifference map, the consumer gets _____.**

    a. the same utility at all the points

    b. more utility when he moves upward to the right

    c. more utility when he moves downward to the left

    d. it does not show utility

7. **Two indifference curves cannot _____.**

   a. intersect

   b. provide the same utility

   c. have a concave shape

   d. all of the above

8. **Any point below the budget line is**

   a. non-feasible for the consumer

   b. feasible for the consumer

   c. only feasible for luxury goods

   d. only feasible for inferior goods

9. **When the consumer's purchases are below the budget line, he will have**

   a. positive savings

   b. zero savings

   c. unrelated to savings

   d. both b and c

10. **Indifference curves cannot be concave in nature as that shows:**

   a. Consumption of more amount of goods gives the same satisfaction as the consumption of less amount of goods

   b. Marginal utility of demand is established

   c. Utility is not related to price

   d. None of the above

Answers	1 – b	2 – c	3 – a	4 – c	5 – a
	6 – b	7 – d	8 – b	9 – a	10 – a

Chapter **6**

Theory of Cost and Production

In this chapter, the readers are introduced to the essential theories of cost and production. We consume a lot of products as consumers and contribute to production as a farmer, a baker, or an artist, producing vegetables, bread, or music. This chapter outlines` the meaning of production, and explains the concepts of inputs and outputs, economies of scale, and returns to scale. There are various inputs needed for production and the cost of these inputs needs to be considered. The chapter discusses the cost of production and analyzes components like fixed and variable costs.

Key learning objectives of this chapter include the reader's understanding of the following:

- Concept of production and the theory of production function

- How the input-output relationship is established

- Concept of the total, average, and marginal products

- Various types of returns to scale like constant, decreasing and increasing returns to scale

- Concept of economies of scale

- Concept of cost of production

- Components of cost, like fixed cost and variable cost

6.1 Meaning of Production

Every morning, Melinda gets up, brushes her teeth, and exercises in a local gym, followed by breakfast at home with bread, butter, and coffee. Now the toothbrush, toothpaste, fitness training, bread, butter, and coffee all are produced by different people. While toothbrushes and toothpastes are manufactured products, fitness training is a service, and the bread, butter, and coffee are produced by the joint efforts of the manufacturing sector and the farm sector. All these products are end results of the production system. We consume a lot of products as consumers and contribute to the production process as workers in various sectors. A country's Gross Domestic Product (GDP) is the total goods or services produced within the country in a given year. We can expand the GDP by producing more, leading to more income for the people and prosperity for the country.

While production is important for society, the choice of production technique depends on the availability of the factors of production and their related costs. A fabric manufacturing unit in India or Bangladesh may adopt hand-driven looms with hundreds of laborers, while in Switzerland, the fabric may be manufactured with high-speed automated looms with the latest robotic techniques that employ very less manpower. Why does Bangladesh or India adopt labor-intensive industries? Can they not manufacture or import automated looms? Certainly, they can! But it is a matter of choice. Due to the availability of an abundant labor force, it is cost-effective for them to adopt labor-intensive technologies. With high labor costs and availability of capital at low-interest rates, for Switzerland or Germany technology-driven capital-intensive techniques are more cost-effective. Cost is a major determinant of the production technique. It answers one of our central problems of the economy, i.e., 'How to Produce'? In a free market, without any restriction on the movement of goods, the cost of production determines which items can be produced in which parts of the world so that consumers across the globe can get the products at the cheapest price.

In this chapter, we focus on the basic economics of cost and production.

6.2 Input and Output

Wheat and labor are inputs for the production of bread. Bread is the final output. A fabric-producing textile mill needs inputs like cotton, dyes, and various chemicals. With labor and machines, these inputs are transformed into fabric rolls. There is a relationship between inputs and outputs. A certain amount of inputs required for obtaining an amount of output is what we call the production function. The production function establishes the relationship between inputs and outputs.

In the words of Samuelson and Nordhaus, "The production function specifies the maximum output that can be produced with a given quantity of inputs. It is defined as a given state of engineering and technical knowledge"[55].

In a large automobile factory, there are different shop floors producing different components. Some of the components like gearboxes are sourced as ready components from an original equipment manufacturer (OEM), while the rest are made in the factory and then assembled. Different shopfloor units have different needs concerning the type and quantity of raw materials. There are various categories of workers like skilled and unskilled workers and supervisors. There are departments like the quality assurance department and research and development. All of these are the inputs to produce the final output, i.e., the motor car. There are millions of dollars of investment involved in the setting up of a factory. Involvement of all the factors of production[56] like land, labor, capital, and entrepreneurship are seen in this factory. The productivity of the factory determines how efficiently the setup uses various inputs to deliver the final output of the motor car.

6.3 Total, Marginal and Average Product

When we consider a firm's total production, the total units produced in a given amount of time is the total production. Now, we know that the word 'marginal' means extra. When we have the total production for a given input, we can calculate the change in total production with the addition of an extra unit of input. This extra unit of production out of an additional unit of input

---

55. Samuelson, P. A., & Nordhaus, W. D. (2009). Economics 19e.p 108.

56. Land, labor, capital and entrepreneurship are factors of production. However, for convenience, often economists club land and entrepreneurship with capital and we consider two factors of production; labor and capital.

is the **marginal product**. Samuelson and Nordhaus, define it as: "The **marginal product** of an input is the extra output produced by 1 additional unit of that input while other inputs are held constant"[57]. The average product is the total product divided by the total number of inputs.

Table 6.1 presents a situation in a hypothetical garment factory. When they employ 1 unit of labor, a lot of machines remain idle and the total production is only 12 units in a week. This increases with the addition of labor in the factory. Initially, the marginal product is high, which reduces with the addition of labor, and finally at some point, the marginal product becomes negative. Marginal products can be negative when the additional labor does not have anything positive to contribute to the output. There may not be adequate raw material or machines which can complement the productivity of the extra worker; rather it may have a negative effect.

Table 6.1 **Total, Marginal and Average products**

No of laborers	No of garments produced; Total Products (TP)	Marginal Products (MP)	Average Product
1	12	12	12
2	36	24	18
3	69	33	23
4	108	39	27
5	150	42	30
6	192	42	32
7	231	39	33
8	264	33	33
9	288	24	32
10	300	12	30
11	297	-3	27
12	276	-21	23

57. Samuelson, P. A., & Nordhaus, W. D. (206.09). Economics 19e.p 108.

Figure 6.1   Total Output

No of garments produced; Total Products (TP)

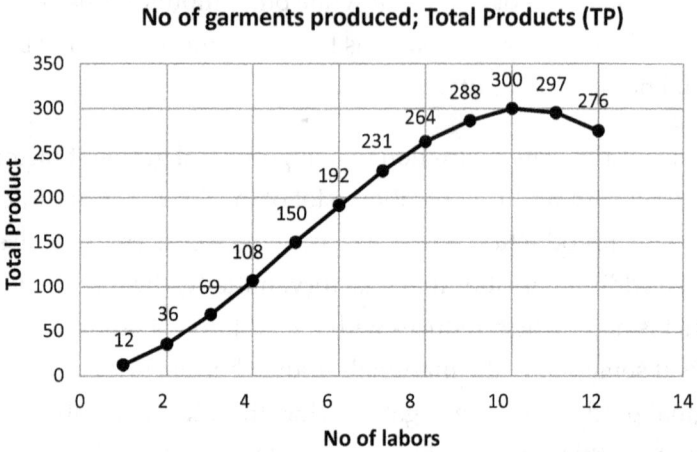

Figure 6.2   Marginal and Average Product

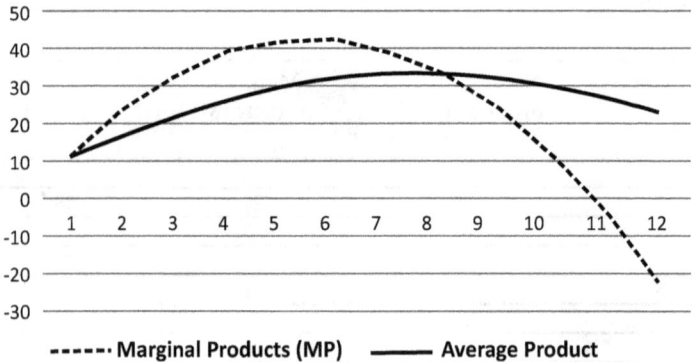

------ Marginal Products (MP)   —— Average Product

6.4 Returns to Scale

In a production process, there are multiple inputs like labor, capital, land, raw material, intermediates, etc. When we produce wheat, labor is one of the inputs, but the production is also dependent on other inputs like land, fertilizer, water, tractors, etc. Now, the diminishing returns seen above is the response of output to the change in a single input (in this case, labor) when all other inputs remain constant. Now, we are interested in seeing the effect of all inputs on the final output. In an automobile factory, if we increase the labor, space for factory shade, assembly lines, and supply of components by 100 percent, what will be the effect on output? Will it go up by 100 percent, 50 percent, or 120 percent? If the farmer gets more seed, more land, and more fertilizers, how will the output of wheat change? From here, we get into three different situations; constant returns to scale, increasing returns to scale (often termed as economies of scale), and decreasing returns to scale. In the words of Samuelson and Nordhaus[58], "Production shows increasing, decreasing, or constant returns to scale when a balanced increase in all inputs leads to a more-than-proportional, less than-proportional, or just-proportional increase in output".

Constant Return to Scale

It is a situation in which we observe proportionate changes in the output when all inputs are increased equally. In this case, when land, labor, and capital are doubled, production is also doubled. So, in the case of an automobile factory, when labor, space for factory shade, assembly lines, and supply of components double, the number of cars produced also doubles.

---

58. Samuelson, P. A., & Nordhaus, W. D. (2009). Economics 19e.p 111.

Constant returns are observed in the case of a beauty salon or in a garment factory where an increase in output is proportionate to the increase in inputs.

Increasing Returns to Scale

In the case of many manufacturing industries like chemicals, fertilizers, etc., it is observed that a change in inputs increases the outputs more than the proportionate level. In this kind of industry, it is important for the manufacturer to increase the output, else they will become uncompetitive. The increased inputs and more than proportionate outputs lead to an efficient production system.

Decreasing returns to scale

In this case, an increase in all inputs leads to a less than proportionate increase in the output. When the input increases by 10 percent, the returns can be 5 percent or 8 percent but always will remain below 10 percent. This kind of return is observed in organizations where the overheads or costs of management are very high. Often public sector enterprises under government control suffer from this as the cost of control and bureaucracy is high.

6.5 Economies of Scale

Productivity is the ratio of outputs to inputs. Usually, the total input is calculated as a weighted average of all the inputs. The weights are assigned as per their importance in the production process. In agricultural production, water may have a higher weightage than pesticides. Now, productivity depends on technology, process innovation, and product innovation. In the case of increasing returns to scale, a larger amount of inputs will enable one to achieve higher productivity.

Economies of scale are the cost advantages that enterprises achieve due to their scale of operation. When an enterprise reaches economies of scale, its cost per unit output comes down due to increased productivity and reduced cost[59]. Economies of scale are important for the organization if it wants to achieve higher productivity. The world economy, particularly the advanced economies, has witnessed high productivity during the last two decades, due to technological changes and digital transformations. This has made economies of scale even more important for organizations. Multinational corporations like Unilever, Coke, or software giants like Google and Microsoft have achieved large economies of scale and higher productivity.

---

59. Samuelson, P. A., & Nordhaus, W. D. (2009). Economics 19e.p 660.

6.6 Cost of Production

Production and costs are strongly related. Without estimating costs, one cannot think about the production process. Firms need to pay for all their inputs. Raw material components, labor, and electricity all cost money. The importance of cost is not limited to calculating profitability. It determines investment decisions. Often, companies decide whether to stick with a business or not depending on the cost factor. Organizations decide on their locational choice of production based on costs. If Apple has to decide whether to shift some of its production to China or India, the cost is a major factor influencing that decision. Companies may outsource some of their processes to low-cost countries to save on costs.

Dwivedi[60] writes that "The money value of inputs and outputs are called the ***cost of production*** and ***revenue***". When the cost of production is deducted from the revenue, we get the profits for the business operation. It shows why the firm is in business.

The cost of production can be divided into various components like labor costs, material costs, operational costs, administrative costs, and overhead costs. There are also concepts like business costs and full costs. While business costs are the costs of operation, including all expenses towards the operation and the depreciation of machinery, the full cost includes the opportunity cost and normal profit. Opportunity cost is the income that could be obtained out of the second-best option available for the entrepreneur, often calculated based on the entrepreneur's service

---

60. Dwivedi, D. N. (2016). Microeconomics: Theory and Applications.p.244. Vikas Publishing House

costs and costs of capital. Normal profit is the minimum earning which is necessary to justify the continuation of the business.

Without understanding the cost of production, the theory of production will be incomplete. In the next few sections, we will focus on various types of costs.

6.7 Total Cost, Fixed Cost, and Variable Cost

The firm can classify its total costs of operation into fixed and variable costs. Fixed costs are those costs that remain the same irrespective of the level of output of the firm. A firm needs to pay rent for its premises. Even if it has zero production in a month, the cost of rent remains the same as a fixed cost. During the lockdown related to the pandemic, a lot of firms ran out of business due to high fixed costs that they had to pay despite zero or limited levels of output. Fixed costs include the salary of the managerial and administrative staff and the depreciation of assets and machinery. Variable costs are those costs that vary with the amount of output. Raw material consumption happens only when there is production. A garment factory will use fabric, its raw material, only when the garments are produced. Part of the electricity expenses are directly proportional to the run time of the machines and varies directly with the output. However, some part of it may be consumed in the office for the functioning of the administrative staff. So, costs like electricity may be divided into both fixed and variable costs.

Total costs represent the total cost incurred in achieving a certain level of output. With the increase in output, the total costs will go up. Now, by definition:

Total cost (TC) = Total variable cost (TVC) + Total fixed cost (TFC)

TFC is unaffected by the quantity of output; the firm will incur this cost even when production is zero.

Table 6.2	Fixed Cost, Variable Cost, and Total Cost

Quantity (q)	Fixed Cost, FC (in $)	Variable Cost, VC (in $)	Total Cost, TC (in $)
0	110	0	110
1	110	60	170
2	110	110	220
3	110	150	260
4	110	210	320
5	110	310	420
6	110	450	560

When we refer to table 6.2, we see that fixed costs remain the same for zero units of production as well as 6 units of production. However, the variable cost keeps increasing with an increase in the output quantity. Total cost also moves upward with the increase in output.

Total, Average and Marginal Costs

Now average cost is a statistical function, rather than the actual cost. Suppose, we produce a quantity Q at a cost of TC, then the average cost (AC) will be

$$AC = TC / Q$$

Marginal cost is the addition to the total cost when we produce an extra unit of output.

Marginal Cost (MC) = Δ TC/Δ TQ

Marginal cost is an important concept in economics. "Marginal cost (MC) denotes the extra or additional cost of producing 1 extra unit of output"[61]. When we refer to Table 6.2, the first unit of production has a marginal cost of $60. Subsequently, the marginal costs change to 50, 40, 70, and 90 with the production of the 2nd, 3rd, 4th and 5th units respectively.

Table 6.3	**Marginal Cost**

Quantity	Total Cost (in $)	Marginal Cost (in $)
0	110	0
1	170	60
2	220	50
3	260	40
4	320	70
5	420	90
6	560	140

61. Samuelson, P. A., & Nordhaus, W. D. (2009). Economics 19e.p 127.

| Figure 6.3 | Total Cost (in $) |

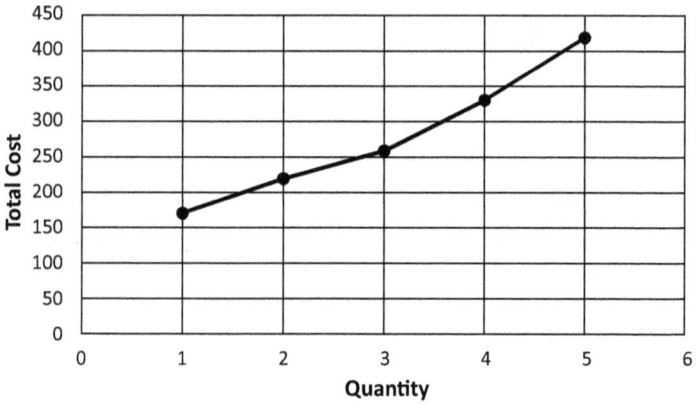

| Figure 6.4 | Marginal Cost with Quantity |

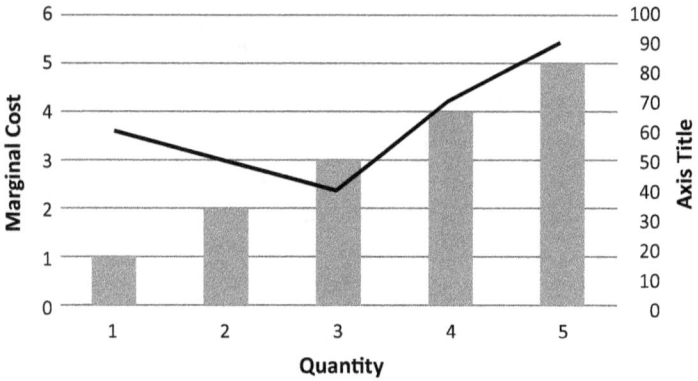

Figure 6.5	**Average Cost (in $)**

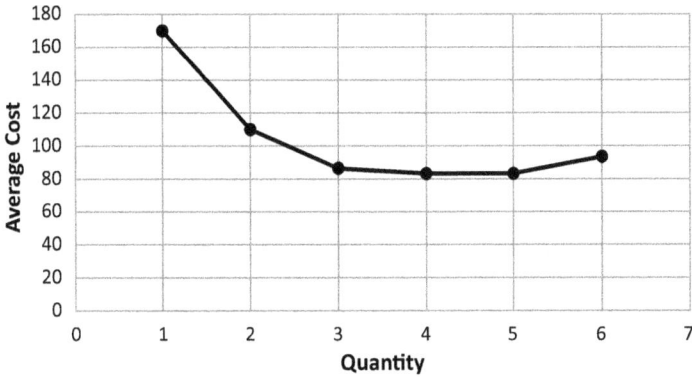

In the case of Total cost in Figure 6.3, we observe that it is increasing with the increase in output although the rate of increase is not uniform. The marginal cost of the firm initially falls and then rises again, as is evident in figure 6.4.

The average fixed cost of the firm will fall with an increase in the quantity of output; however, the variable cost does not decrease with an increase in the quantity. The marginal cost diminishes initially and then rises again. This is shown in the average cost curve in figure 6.5, where the average cost drops initially and then again starts rising after a certain production point.

The calculation of various types of costs enables us to determine the optimal production quantity.

Discussion Questions

1. Explain economies of scale in the context of price of a meal at McDonald's in comparison to a restaurant.

2. How does the unit fixed cost decrease when we increase the operations in a factory from 2 shifts to 3 shifts?

Chapter Summary

♦ We consume a lot of products as consumers and contribute to the production process as workers in various sectors.

♦ The choice of production technique depends on the availability of the factors of production and the related costs.

♦ Cost is a major determinant of the production technique.

♦ The production function specifies the maximum output that can be produced with a given quantity of inputs

♦ This extra production out of an additional unit of input is the marginal product, all other inputs held constant.

♦ Average product is the total product divided by the total number of inputs.

♦ When more than one input item increases, we have a constant, increasing, and diminishing rate of returns.

♦ An increasing rate of return is also termed as economies of scale.

♦ Organizations try to achieve economies of scale to become competitive in the market.

♦ Productivity is the ratio of output to input.

♦ Economies of scale are important for the organization to achieve higher productivity.

♦ The productivity of the factory determines how efficiently the setup uses various inputs to deliver the final output.

◆ Total cost has two components: total fixed cost and total variable cost.

◆ Fixed cost does not change with the quantity of output, but variable cost changes with the quantity of output.

◆ Marginal cost (MC) denotes the extra or additional cost of producing 1 extra unit of output.

◆ The average fixed cost of a production unit decreases with an increase in the quantity of output.

Quiz

1. **Productivity depends on _____.**

   a. output

   b. input

   c. both a and b

   d. none of the above

2. **Economies of scale means _____.**

   a. constant returns to scale

   b. decreasing returns to scale

   c. increasing returns to scale

   d. none of the above

3. **Choice of production technique depends on _____.**

   a. availability and price of labor

   b. availability and price of capital

   c. accepted industry norms

   d. options a and b

4. **The marginal product curve _____ with a change in quantity.**

   a. increases initially and then decreases

   b. decreases initially and then increases

   c. continuously increases

   d. continuously decreases

5. **The average cost is defined as _____.**

   a. total cost divided by the quantity of output

   b. total cost divided by the quantity of inputs

   c. total cost divided by marginal cost

   d. marginal cost divided by the quantity of output

6. **Identify the false statement.**

   a. The price of all inputs determines the cost of the product

   b. Revenue is the product of output and price

   c. Constant returns to scale is the ideal situation for an expansion

   d. Increasing returns to scale is the ideal situation for an expansion

7. In a factory, the total product changes from 170 units to 210 units when the total labor is changed from 10 to 11. The marginal product is

    a. 40

    b. 4

    c. 1

    d. 20

8. The fixed cost for producing 10 units of garments is $10,000. The management increases the production to 100 units. The average fixed cost will be

    a. $100

    b. $1000

    c. $10

    d. Cannot be determined

9. In a particular automobile unit, labor, factory space, raw material, and assembly lines capacity are all increased by 2.5 times. The factory was earlier producing 20 vehicles per day and it increases its production now to 50 vehicles per day. The returns to scale are ___ ___.

    a. constant

    b. increasing

    c. decreasing

    d. cannot be determined

10. The fixed cost for a production unit is $1,00,000. When the output increases from 60 units to 120 units, the total fixed cost will change to _____.

   a. $200000

   b. $50000

   c. $5000

   d. will not change

Answers	1 – c	2 – c	3 – d	4 – a	5 – a
	6 – c	7 – a	8 – a	9 – a	10 – d

Chapter 7

Market

This chapter introduces the reader to the concept of a market and its features. It outlines various forms of markets like monopoly, duopoly, oligopoly, monopsony, pure competition, and perfect competition. It introduces the readers to the concepts of monopolistic competition and price discrimination.

Key learning objectives of this chapter include the reader's understanding of the following:

- Concept of markets

- How the various forms of market structures are created

- How the market functions under the structures of monopoly, duopoly, oligopoly, and monopsony

- Concepts of pure competition and perfect competition

- Concept of monopolistic competition

- How price discrimination works for the marketer

7.1 What is a Market?

A market is a place where buyers and sellers meet for transactions. A retail mall is a place where lots of buyers meet sellers of various brands within a given day. It is not necessarily a physical marketplace but can also be a virtual platform. In the stock market, both buyers and sellers are behind their computer screens, meeting on a virtual platform. Amazon provides a virtual marketplace to its online buyers.

7.2 Various Forms of Market

Market structure is the organizational structure of an industry that determines the price and output of the products offered. The market structure depends on the number of sellers and buyers in a market. Sellers' and buyers' behavior varies depending on the number of sellers or buyers in the market and the competition between the sellers. The distinctiveness of the product, price elasticity, control of the price, and distribution are various variables that determine the characteristics of the market. There are various forms of markets like monopoly, duopoly, oligopoly, monopsony, pure competition, and perfect competition. Monopolistic competition, which is also a form of market, allows product differentiation and the creation of unique products. The uniqueness of the product creates the opportunity of increasing the price for the seller.

In general, the market structure is generally classified into perfect competition and imperfect competition.

7.2.1. Perfect Competition

Perfect competition is an idealized form of the market with a large number of buyers and sellers offering homogenous products.

As the sellers are very large and the product is homogenous without the scope of differentiation in value offered, the firms are price takers. They are bound to sell at the price determined by the market. The demand curves for each seller are horizontal with elasticity being infinite ($E = \infty$), meaning that a firm can sell any amount at a market-determined price. However, in the real world, we do not see perfect competition and the concept is more hypothetical and of theoretical interest. In the real world, we see a few large firms dominating the entire market. Take the examples of Mcdonald's, Ford, Toyota, and Coke, which all dominate the market and compete with a few large companies. In the world of the web, we see a few search engines like Bing, Yahoo, and Google, where Google is dominating the market. In the market of social media, Meta under the brand name of Facebook and Instagram is enjoying almost a monopoly.

The closest example of perfect competition is the market for cereals, pulses, or vegetables in which a large number of sellers offer similar products to a large number of buyers.

From the above discussion, we understand that perfect competition has the following main characteristics:

a. It has a large number of buyers

b. The product offered is homogenous

c. There are a very large number of sellers in the market

In addition, perfect competition has the following important characteristics:

d. The factors of production have perfect mobility

For production, firms need labor and capital. The cost of these factors varies across the world. Perfect mobility means no firm has control over the labor and capital and they can move from one firm to another freely. In a world with restrictions on passports and visas, perfect mobility of labor is hypothetical. There are barriers like skillsets, language, distance, and legalities that prohibit the movement of labor. Capital movements are also subject to restrictions in many countries. However, in perfect competition, the factors of production, namely land, labor, and capital have perfect mobility.

e. There is free entry and free exit for the firms in the market

In perfect competition, the firms are able to enter the industry without any restrictions and can also leave the market at their will. However, in reality, there are legal and social barriers for entry and exit for companies. Under perfect competition, firms are able to enter an industry that has more potential for profit and they may also leave when profits do not meet their expectations of return on investment (ROI).

f. There is perfect knowledge

It is assumed that all players in the market have perfect knowledge and information about the prices, availability of the products, and market conditions, without any uncertainty.

g. There is no Government interference

In perfect competition, there is no government interference in the functioning of the market. There are no discriminatory taxes, subsidies, or licensing systems for firms.

h. There is independent decision-making by firms, without forming any cartel

The organization for Oil Producing and Exporting Countries (OPEC) has 13 prominent oil-producing countries as its members, which often influence the output and price of oil. Perfect competition does not allow these kinds of cartels. It also does not allow any kind of activism by the buyer's associations, like campaigns by the environmentalists against a specific company. This characteristic implies independent decision-making by both buyers and sellers.

Perfect competition without the characteristics of perfect mobility of factors of production is termed as Pure Competition. This is termed 'pure' as there is no element of monopoly in it.

7.2.2. Imperfect Competition

Imperfect competition, which is more prevalent in real life, has various forms like monopoly, duopoly, and oligopoly.

In the words of Dwivedi, "Imperfect competition is said to exist when a number of firms sell identical or differentiated products with some control over the price of their product."[62]

Imperfect competition takes place due to barriers to entry for the firms in a market or industry. Patents, for example, can exclude new entrants from the market. Companies can continue with a price advantage till the time the patent expires. Often, large companies reach economies of scale and new entrants cannot compete with them. Their cost of production becomes low due to economies of scale and the entry of new firms becomes unviable. In some countries, permission from the government is required, in the form of licenses, to enter a specific market. There can also be legal barriers to exclude firms from an industry, leading to imperfect competition.

62. Dwivedi, D. N. (2016). Microeconomics: Theory and Applications.p.290. Vikas Publishing House.

Table 7.1	**Various Market Structures**

Type of Markets	Number of firms in the market	Number of buyers	Product type	Firms' control on price of the product
Perfect competition	Many	Many	Homogeneous (Cereal, pulses, vegetables)	No control
Imperfect competition				
Monopoly	One	Many	Government service	Full control
Duopoly	Two	Many	Soft beverages- Coke and Pepsi	Partial control
Oligopoly	Few	Many	Computer, Cars, Gasoline	Limited control
Monopolistic competition	Many	Many	Toothbrush, cosmetics	Partial control
Monopsony	Many	One	A tea garden buying labor of local workers	Complete control

7.2.3 Monopoly

In perfect competition, we have a large number of sellers. Monopoly is a diametrically opposite concept to perfect competition. In a monopoly market, there is only one seller. In perfect competition, as there is a large number of sellers, no one dictates the price. All the sellers in perfect competition are price takers and not price makers; in contrast to that, in a monopoly market, the seller has complete power to decide the price of the product. One important characteristic of a monopoly is that it belongs to a single-firm industry. There is no other member of the industry, hence there is no difference between the firm's demand

and industry demand. In this section, we will discuss a few important concepts associated with a monopoly market.

Competition in Monopoly

The above paragraph must not lead to any misconception that monopoly is free from any competition. There is indirect competition in a monopoly market. There can be substitute goods offered in the market which will compete with the product supplied by the monopoly. If in a country, Uber is the only player in the app-based ride-sharing service, there will be competition from other transport services like city bus services.

How is Monopoly Established?

While monopoly is seldom seen in the modern economic system, there are few instances of near-monopoly power. There can be legal rights conferred to an electrical distribution company by a local authority for a particular place. This will create a situation in which there is a monopoly by the seller. In a large country like India, the entire railway operation is managed by the government and it is an example of a monopoly. Intellectual property rights often allow a particular company to have entire selling rights. This is prevalent in the pharmaceutical industry. GlaxoSmithKline[63] (GSK) was the first company to develop the treatment for HIV and had the entire right to produce and distribute this medication. When a company acquires the right to a key natural resource, it is able to create monopoly power. It has been witnessed in the case of the steel and aluminum industry in America. Research & Development enables firms to create monopoly power in the market. The best examples are Microsoft

---

63. Read more at https://www.gsk.com/en-gb/about-us/our-history/creating-the-gsk-of-today-1950-1999/

Windows and the search engine Google. The competitors for them are marginal, allowing almost complete monopoly power. To restrict monopoly power, the US has antitrust laws.

7.2.4 Oligopoly

Oligopoly is an example of imperfect competition. It is a market condition in which there are a few sellers. It indicates rivalry among a few players in the industry. The literature on economics has not specified the maximum number of firms that can exist in an oligopoly. The lower limit is two, which indicates the condition of a duopoly.

In an oligopoly, firms can sell homogeneous or differentiated products. When the firms sell homogeneous products, they are termed as homogenous oligopolies. Cooking gas, electricity, gasoline, and cement are examples of homogenous oligopolies. When the products are differentiated it is called heterogeneous oligopoly; examples are refrigerators, air conditioners, computers, and cigarettes.

How is Oligopoly Established?

In certain industries, there are requirements for large investments which deter the entry of many sellers. A certain scale of economy is essential for gaining cost advantages, so only the player who can have large-scale production can survive in certain industries. The economies of scale achieved by the existing firms work as a barrier for the new entrants. Capability for large investments and economies of scale create a comparative advantage for a few. Intellectual property rights also create an advantage for some firms in the case of a differentiated oligopoly. The entry is restricted to only those who have patented products in these categories. As we saw in the case of monopoly, in oligopoly too, a few firms may have more control over the raw materials and create entry barriers for new entrants. Often, license requirements for imported raw materials or in-house production through backward integration give some firms easier and cheaper access to raw materials and keep the cost of production lower.

7.2.5 Duopoly

It is the simplest form of oligopoly with two sellers. Samuelson[64] considers the example of shuttle services between New York and Washington. The route was served by Delta and US Airways. Now, if one of them reduces the price, the other one will have to match this price reduction. If they do not have any kind of understanding among them, they will need to make an educated guess about the pricing of the other. Coke and Pepsi are the main suppliers of soft drinks across the world in many markets. The size of the market they cater to with their multiple brands is so large, that they have established a duopoly with control over the market prices. The classic case of 'prisoners' dilemma' is used by Rittenberg and Tregarthen[65] to explain the strategy in the case of a duopoly. Two prisoners involved in the same crime are caught and interrogated separately. If they both do not accept their crime, together they will be better off with lighter sentences. However, if one of them accepts it, their sentences will be more. But without any interaction in the secluded cell, they may choose the wrong strategy.

---

64. Samuelson, P. A., & Nordhaus, W. D. (2009). Economics 19e.p 193

65. Rittenberg, L., & Tregarthen, T. (2013). Principles of Microeconomics: Saylor.p 273

Suppose an industry has a duopoly. Figure 7.1 shows a case in which two firms are selling identical products and have the same cost and demand curves.

To keep the analysis simple, we consider the marginal cost curve MC as horizontal.

Figure 7.1 **Duopoly of firms: Price and Marginal Revenue**

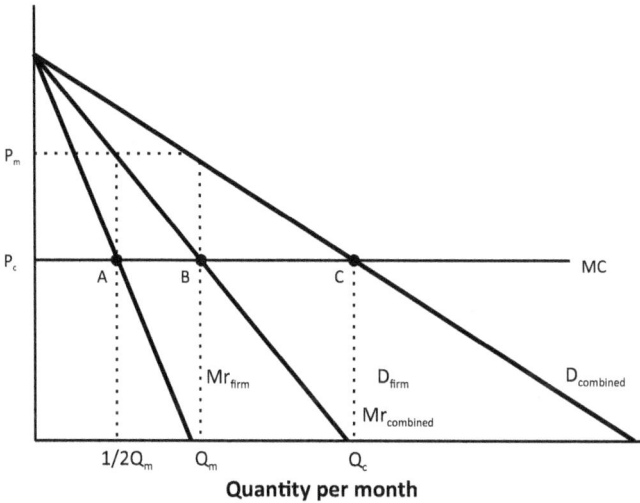

In figure 7.1, the combined demand curve is D and the combined marginal revenue is $MR_{combined}$

Now, the individual firms will maximize their profits at a price Pm and quantity $Q_m/2$. The industry output will be at point B at quantity Q_m and price P_m. The efficiency level is highest at point C when price equals MC and total quantity is Q_c.

Firms often openly agree on a collusion or understanding of prices for earning profits. We have seen the example of a cartel in the case of OPEC countries. However, a cartel for earning monopoly profits is not an easy option for the firms. They are banned in many countries including the USA. Their restrictions on output and maximizing profit are often considered illegal. Secondly, all firms in the industry may not join the cartel. The firm outside the cartel reduces its market price. Some firms may betray the cartel after joining it.

7.2.6 Monopsony

Rittenberg and Tregarthen[66] define monopsony as "Monopsony is the buyer's counterpart of monopoly. Monopoly means a single seller; monopsony means a single buyer." Samuelson and Nordhaus[67] explain monopsony as "The mirror image of monopoly: a market in which there is a single buyer; a "buyer's monopoly." While in monopoly, we have a single seller, in a monopsony, we have a single buyer. Monopsony is often seen in the factor market. Suppose a city has a single mine, so all mining laborers have only one place to sell their labor. A tea garden in a locality will be the only source of employment for the tea garden workers in that locality. This is a form of monopsony. There is a close resemblance in the functioning of monopsony and monopoly. In both cases, the firms are price makers having the monopoly power.

7.3 Monopolistic Competition

In monopolistic competition, a large number of sellers produce differentiated products. Similar to perfect competition, monopolistic competition has a large number of sellers. However,

---

66. Rittenberg, L., & Tregarthen, T. (2013). Principles of Microeconomics: Saylor.p 741

67. Samuelson, P. A., & Nordhaus, W. D. (2009). Economics 19e.p 668

unlike perfect competition, here products are not homogenous. In differentiated products, the important product features vary. For example, there are a large number of sellers of mobile phones across the world. The features of the phones vary from brand to brand. The camera, screen size, processor, and operating system all determine the phone's demand and price. Though it is the same product, utility varies depending on the features. Quality is an important determinant for product differentiation. Buyers' segments vary depending on the product quality. Brands like iPhone can create a monopoly-like advantage within the market with their product features and quality.

7.4 Price Discrimination

In a monopoly, the seller has the power to charge different prices to different sets of buyers. When different buyers pay different prices for an identical product, it is termed **price discrimination.**

However, price discrimination is not applicable only in the case of a monopoly market. Price discrimination is seen in various oligopolistic markets as well. Airlines charge different prices depending on the time of booking. If you book in advance, you pay less. If you buy a ticket on the day of the journey, you may be charged more. Age is also often a determinant of price. Museums often have concessionary tickets for school children. Universities have different fee structures for foreign students, which is often more compared to the fees for domestic students. During the peak season, hotel fares skyrocket, while the same room is offered at a discount during the off-season.

Price discrimination allows the seller to cater to different segments and maximize his revenue.

We take a simple example of an airline that can sell tickets as per Table 7.2.

Table 7.2   Price Discrimination by an Airline company

Case I	No of tickets	Price in USD	Revenue at a price point
Fixed price	120	100	12,000
	Total Revenue		12,000
Case II			
Variable Price	70	70	4900
	50	100	5000
	20	120	2400
	Total Revenue		12,300
Case III			
Fixed Price	150	80	12,000
	Total Revenue		12,000

In case I, airlines kept the fixed price at $100 and could sell only 120 seats. In case III when the price is dropped to $80, its sales go up to 150 seats. The market is price elastic, so the revenue in both cases remains the same. In case II when it adopts price discrimination, the total revenue is $12,300. This gives the airlines the opportunity to serve various types of buyers at different price points. However, price discrimination does not always mean revenue maximization. The pricing technique determines the total revenue and profits. The pricing decisions are taken considering the market condition, price elasticity of demand, and the competitors' prices.

Discussion Questions

1. What is a monopoly power? How can branding create monopolistic power for a company? Discuss with an example of a specific brand.

2. Is perfect competition a myth? Justify your statement with an analysis of the market condition of your country.

Chapter Summary

◆ The market structure is the organizational structure of an industry that determines the price and output of the products offered.

◆ The various forms of markets are monopoly, duopoly, oligopoly, monopsony, pure competition, and perfect competition.

◆ By definition, perfect competition has a large number of buyers offering homogenous products to a large number of sellers.

◆ Perfect competition ensures the mobility of labor and capital within the industry and free entry and exit of the firms.

◆ Monopolistic competition has firms with unique products and allows them to create a market through product differentiation.

◆ In a monopoly market, there is only one seller.

◆ Oligopoly, an example of imperfect competition is a market condition in which there are a few sellers. It indicates rivalry among a few players in the industry.

◆ When different buyers pay different prices for an identical product, it is termed price discrimination.

Quiz

1. **In perfect competition, firms are _____.**

    a. price-makers

    b. price takers

    c. both a and be

    d. neither a nor b

2. **Under perfect competition, it is assumed that _____.**

    a. labor is mobile but capital is not

    b. capital is mobile but labor is not

    c. both are mobile

    d. none of the above

3. **In case of monopoly:**

    a. Firms do not have any competition

    b. Firms have an internal competition to excel

    c. Firms compete with substitute goods

    d. None ot the above

4. **In the cement industry in a country, there are 12 main players along with a few unorganized players, which is an example of _____.**

    a. monopolistic competition

    b. oligopoly

    c. perfect competition

    d. none of the above

5. **In perfect competition, firms can _____.**

    a. enter and exit the industry at any point

    b. there is a restriction on entry but not on exit

    c. there is a restriction on exit but not on entry

    d. there is price control by the state

6. **In monopoly and monopsony, the price is decided by the _____.**

    a. buyer in both the cases

    b. seller in both the cases

    c. seller in former and buyer in later

    d. the market

7. **Cartel is a market condition which is _____.**

    a. profitable for the firms but is unethical

    b. not profitable

    c. possible only with permission from the authorities

    d. neither profitable nor legal

8. **In a monopolistic market, firms can become _____.**

    a. price-makers due to product differentiation

    b. price takers due to product differentiation

    c. price-makers due to price differentiation

    d. they are neither price-makers nor price takers

9. **Monopsony is an example of _____.**

    a. perfect competition

    b. imperfect competition

    c. it can be both

    d. it is neither perfect nor imperfect competition

10. Price discrimination helps the firms in _____.

    a. maximizing revenue

    b. minimizing cost

    c. catering to various segments at different prices

    d. both a and c

Answers	1 – b	2 – c	3 – a	4 – b	5 – a
	6 – c	7 – a	8 – a	9 – b	10 – d

Chapter **8**

Theory of a Firm

This chapter introduces the readers to the core theory of firms. The chapter covers the objectives of the firms, and the concept of revenue, costs, and profit. The chapter outlines the concept of short-run and long-run supply curves of a firm and the shutdown point. The chapter explains the concept of normal profit and breakeven point.

Key learning objectives of this chapter include the reader's understanding of the following:

- Objectives of the firm

- Concept of revenue and cost

- How profit is calculated for a firm

- Short-run and long-run supply curves

- Concept of shutdown point

- Concept of breakeven point

8.1 Concept of Firm

A firm is a decision-making unit that transforms the factors of production into finished goods and services for the people. It is an organizational entity employing people for productive purposes that benefit society. In economics, firms include both agricultural firms and industrial firms. In the same way that consumers try to maximize their utility, firms try to maximize their profits or any other objectives they have. Business firms are concerned about profits. Social sector organizations can be not for profit too, with the objective of maximizing social welfare. In our discussion, we mostly concentrate on for-profit firms. Samuelson states that: "Firms maximize profits because that maximizes the economic benefits to the owners of the firm. Allowing lower-than-maximum profits is like asking for a pay cut, which few business owners will voluntarily undertake."[68]

8.2 Concept of Revenue, Cost, and Profit

A firm's top line is the net sales generated by the firm. This is also called the revenue of the firm. Revenue is the product of quantity and price, as we have seen in the previous chapters. Ford produces multiple models of cars, so we take the price for each model and multiply this by the number of cars produced. This product gives us the revenue for a particular model. Now, the grand summation of the revenue of each model will be the company's total revenue, which can be mapped per unit of time. The stock market is interested in knowing the firm's quarterly

---

68. Samuelson, P. A., & Nordhaus, W. D. (2009). Economics 19e.p 150

revenue and yearly revenue to assess its performance. When we deduct the costs incurred by the firms from the total revenue, we get the net profit. Cost, again, has to be calculated for each model and summed up for the entire company. Apart from the production costs, Ford has its administrative expenditure, marketing, and advertising expenses.

Let's assume that Ford produces various models of cars in quantities like $Q_1, Q_2, Q_3, Q_4, \ldots Q_n$. Now if they are sold at price points like $P_1, P_2, P_3, P_4, \ldots P_n$, then,

Total Revenue (TR) = $P_1 \times Q_1 + P_2 \times Q_2 + P_3 \times Q_3 + \ldots P_n \times Q_n$

= $\sum P_i Q_i$ where i = 1 to n

Similarly, the cost function can also be written as TC.

The profit (π) = **TR – TC**

Now in perfect competition, firms can sell any quantity below or at the market price. But the firms will not set the price lower than the market price, as it will lose out on revenue. Hence, the firm will set the price of the product at the level of the market price.

Let's assume that a car manufacturer sells various quantities at different price points, as depicted in Table no 8.1.

Table 8.1   Revenue of an automobile company

Average no of cars sold (in '000)	Average price in USD ($)	USD in million
0	10000	0
10	10000	100
15	10000	150
20	10000	200
25	10000	250
30	10000	300

Figure 8.1   Total Revenue Curve

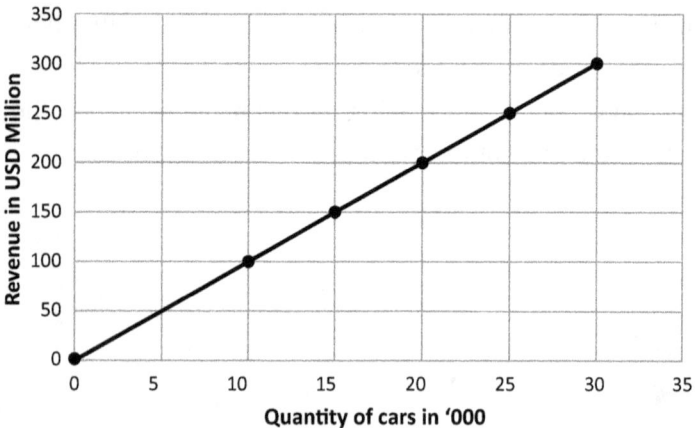

Here in figure 8.1, the total revenue curve is a straight line as the price is constant. The total revenue is 0, when the output is 0, then it rises constantly with output.

Now, the slope of the straight line is the price. Say, at 10,000 unit sales, the slope of the line will be 100,000,000/10,000 = 10,000 ($) which is the price of the car.

It can also be represented as TR = P x Q

Which implies P = TR/ Q.

Figure 8.2   **Average Revenue Curve**

Average Revenue (Price Line)

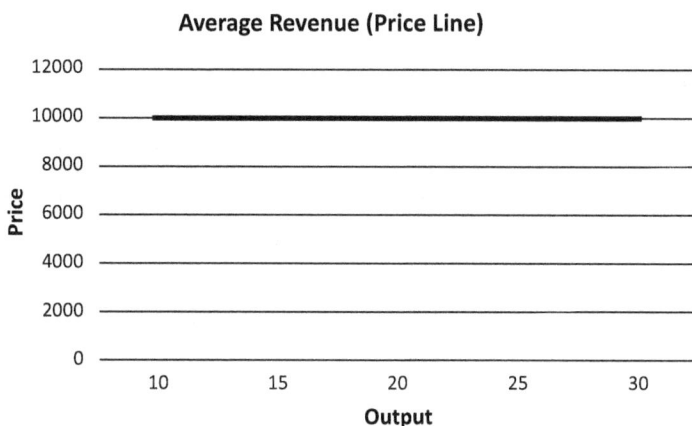

Now, average revenue will be the total revenue divided by the total quantity of output.

Average Revenue (AR) = TR/Q = PQ/Q = P

In figure 8.2, the average revenue curve is the price line set at $10,000, the unit price of the cars.

Marginal revenue (MR) will be the change in revenue due to a unit change in the quantity produced.

Suppose, a firm sells quantity Q1 and quantity Q2, their total revenue (TR) will be TR1 and TR2.

Marginal revenue (MR) = $TR_2 - TR_1 / Q_2 - Q_1$

In the case of our automobile manufacturing company, let's consider, Q2 = 20 (in'000) and Q1 = 15 (in'000) , corresponding revenues are TR2 = 200 (USD Million) and TR1 = 150 (USD Million)

MR = 200000000-150000000/ 20000-15000

   = 50,000,000/ 5,000 = 10,000 ($)

Here, again MR = Price.

So, in the case of a perfectly competitive market, AR = MR = P

We can say that when the firm is a price taker, its average revenue and marginal revenue are equal to the prevailing market price. As the underlying assumption in the case of perfect competition is a constant price irrespective of quantity, any extra unit is sold at the same price, making it possible.

8.3 Profit Maximization

Using profit-maximizing rules, we can find out the profit-maximizing output.[69] There are two conditions in profit-maximizing rules: the first one is a necessary condition and the second one is a supplementary condition. *The necessary condition is that marginal cost (MC) must be equal to marginal revenue (MR).* As long as the MC is lower than MR, the firm will continue making a profit and profit will keep rising. When the MC is at a

---

69. Dwivedi, D. N. (2016). Microeconomics: Theory and Applications.p.283. Vikas Publishing House.

higher level than MR, the profits will start falling. Hence, when MC= MR, the firm reaches the optimum point with maximum profit.

Profit (π) = TR – TC

As a profit-maximizing entity, a firm needs to choose a price and output that maximizes its profit.

Let's assume that TR = 30 Q for a firm and

TC = 80 + 30 Q – 12 Q^2 + Q^3

Now MR = Δ TR/ Δ Q

Implies, MR = 30

MC = Δ TC / Δ Q = 30- 12 Q + 2 Q^2

Profit will be maximum at an output where MC = MR

i.e. 30 = 30- 12 Q + 2 Q^2

i.e. 2 Q^2 – 12 Q = 0

or Q = 6

It means 6 is the optimum output for profit maximization in the above condition.

Figure 8.3   **Optimum output under perfect competition**

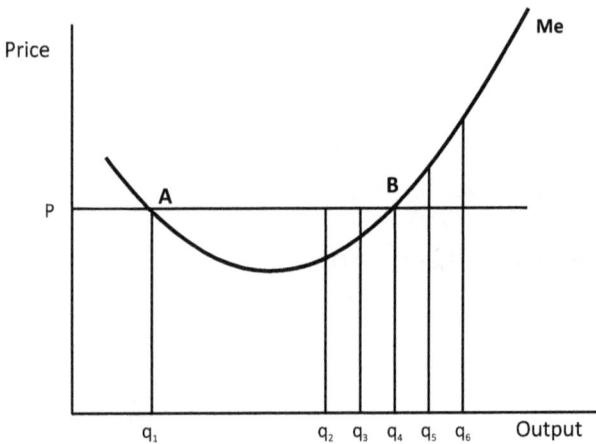

The second-order or supplementary condition is that the first-order condition must be fulfilled when the marginal cost is rising. In the case of figure 8.3., at quantities Q1 and Q4, the price is equal to MC. The quantities on the right side of Q4 are also on the rising MC curve, but they do not fulfill the condition of MR = MC = P. So, the maximum profit will be Q_1 or Q_4. As Q_1 is on the downward slope, the profit-maximizing quantity will be Q_4. At a point slightly before Q1 on the left, the price will be higher than MC, hence, the profit will be slightly more than Q_1. Hence Q_1 is not selected as the profit-maximizing quantity, though it fulfills the condition of MR = MC = P.

8.4 Supply Curve of a Firm

The quantity a firm chooses to sell in the market is the 'Supply'. A table that shows the various quantities a firm supplies at various price points, while all other factors like technology remain the same, is called the 'Supply schedule'. We worked out the supply schedule and supply curve in chapter 2. In this chapter, we will discuss the 'short-run supply' curve and 'long-run supply curve'. There are differences between the supply curve of a firm in the short run and long run as factors like investment and technology may change over time. A profit-maximizing firm reaches the equilibrium quantity when MC = MR. The equilibrium quantity depends on the cost and revenue functions. Cost and revenue functions are dependent on the time period. In the short run, some inputs like capital are constant, while in the long run, all the factors of production may vary.

8.4.1 Short-run supply curve of a firm

In the short run, the firm's capital investment cannot change. However, the total deployment of labor can be changed to alter the production output. While the firm is in short-run equilibrium, a few assumptions are made[70].

1. The firm's input cost is available

2. The firm's product prices are available

3. The firm has a fixed capital and varying labor in the short run

4. The cost curve of the firm in the short run is U-shaped.

Figure 8.4 illustrates the short-run supply curve. In the figure, the price P1 is above the minimum average variable cost (AVC). When we start equating the rising part of the short-run marginal cost curve (SMC curve) with price, we get the output Q_1. The AVC

---

70. Dwivedi, D. N. (2016). Microeconomics: Theory and Applications.p.297. Vikas Publishing House.

is not above the market price, P_1 at the output Q1. Here, both the conditions of profit maximization are fulfilled, i.e. MR = MC =P, and the marginal cost is rising.

At price P_2, the firm's price is below the AVC. A rational firm will not produce at a price that will not cover its variable costs. Hence at any price below the AVC, the production in the short run will remain zero.

Figure 8.4   **Short-run supply curve**

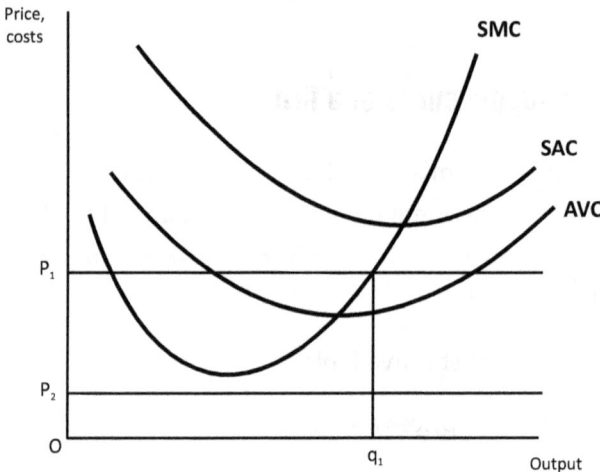

8.4.2 Long-run supply curve of a firm

In the long run, both factors of production, capital, and labor, will vary for the firm.

A factory has a fixed investment in the short run. The capital invested does not vary in the short run. The firm does not change its plan of factory outlay or machinery. But the need for labor is not fixed. It varies with the production targets. If the factory is run for 2 shifts, it has a requirement for a certain number of workers. If the factory gets more orders, the management may decide to run it for three more shifts and the requirement for labor will change.

However, in the long run, depending on the market trends, the factory may require an additional production capacity. This may lead to additional investment for installing more machinery. There will also be a need for more laborers to run the machines.

This way, in the long run, both labor and capital vary, while in the short run, only labor varies.

Figure 8.5 **Long-run supply curve**

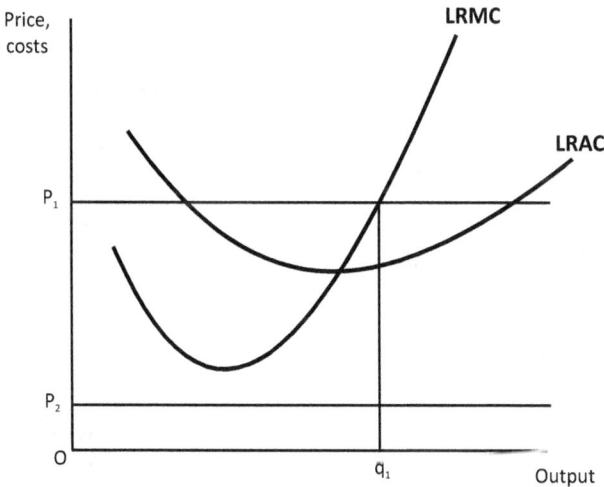

In figure 8.5, The long-run, marginal cost intersects with the price P_1 at the output Q_1. The price point is above the long-run average cost (LRAC) at quantity Q_1. It is fulfilling the conditions for profit maximization i.e. MR = MC =P and the output is in the rising portion of the marginal cost curve.

At price point P_2, the producer will not go for any output as the price is below the average cost curve. Hence, the output will remain zero.

8.4.3 The Shut-Down point

In the short run, a firm will not produce below the minimum point on the AVC, and in the long run, it will not produce below the minimum point on the LRAC. Below the lowest point on AVC, the firm's output will be zero in the short run. In the long run, the output will be zero below the lowest point on LRAC. So, any point below the lowest point of AVC in the short run and below the lowest point on the LRAC is considered shut down points. Samuelson and Nordhaus defined this as, "The critically low market price at which revenues just equal variable costs (or, equivalently, at which losses exactly equal fixed costs) is called the shutdown point"[71]. As per Rittenberg and Tregarthen, "The minimum level of average variable cost, which occurs at the intersection of the marginal cost curve and the average variable cost curve, is called the shutdown point"[72]. The firm will continue its production only at a point above the minimum AVC because as we move down, the last production point will be at the point of minimum AVC where the SMC curve cuts the AVC curve. Similarly, in the long run, the positive production point will be on the LRAC curve and below the LRAC, the production will be shut down.

71. Samuelson, P. A., & Nordhaus, W. D. (2009). Economics 19e.p 153.

72. Rittenberg, L., & Tregarthen, T. (2013). Principles of Microeconomics: Saylor.p 488.

8.4.4 The Normal Profit and Breakeven Point

Normal profit is the minimum level of profit that is needed by a firm to remain in the existing business. If the profit levels are below the normal profit, the firm may exit the industry. Hence, it can be considered as the opportunity cost for the entrepreneur. It is part of the firm's total cost. Any profit above the normal profit is considered to be a supernormal profit. In the long run, a firm will quit if it does not earn a normal profit, however, in the short run it may still produce without earning a normal profit. A point on the supply curve at which a firm earns only normal profit is considered to be the breakeven point. The breakeven point is that point of the minimum average cost curve at which the supply curve cuts the SAC curve in the short-run and LRAC cost in the long run.

Discussion Questions

1. Differentiate between a short-run and a long-run supply curve. Let's assume a hypothetical situation in which Ford invests in Laos and they make capital investment over a period of 5 years in a staggered manner. How will their short-run and long-run supply curve change?

2. Compare between revenue maximization and profit maximization strategies between firms with reference to microeconomic theories.

Chapter Summary

◆ Firms have the objective of profit maximization as that maximizes the economic benefits of the owners of the firms.

◆ The total revenue in excess of the total cost is the profit generated by the firm.

◆ The average revenue of a firm is the price line of the firm.

◆ In the case of a perfectly competitive market, the Average Revenue (AR)= Marginal Revenue (MR) = Price (P).

◆ Under the profit maximization rule, the necessary condition is that marginal cost (MC) must be equal to marginal revenue (MR).

◆ The second-order or supplementary condition is that the first-order condition must be fulfilled when the marginal cost is rising.

◆ There are differences between the supply curve of a firm in the short run and long run, as factors like investment and technology may change over time.

◆ At any price below the AVC, the production in the short run will remain zero.

◆ At any price below the LRAC, the production, in the long run, will remain zero.

◆ The critically low market price at which revenue just equals variable costs is shutdown price. At this point, the fixed cost will be equal to the losses incurred by the firm.

◆ Normal profit is the minimum level of profits that is needed by a firm to remain in the existing business.

◆ Any profit above the normal profit is considered as a supernormal profit.

Quiz

1. **Following are attributes of a firm except**

   a. It is decision making entity

   b. It is an organizational entity

   c. It tries to maximize profit

   d. It has to earn a supernormal profit

2. **Opportunity cost is part of the _____.**

   a. normal profits

   b. supernormal profits

   c. breakeven point

   d. none of the above

3. **Total revenue in excess of the total cost is the _____.**

   a. marginal revenue

   b. average revenue

   c. profit

   d. supernormal profit

4. **Marginal revenue of a firm is the price line in case of**
   _____.

   a. monopoly

   b. oligopoly

   c. imperfect competition

   d. perfect competition

5. **The price remains constant for a firm selling any quantity of goods in the case of _____.**

   a. monopoly

   b. duopoly

   c. monopolistic competition

   d. perfect competition

6. **In perfect competition, under the profit maximization rule:**

   a. The marginal revenue (MR) should be equal to price

   b. The average revenue (AR) should be equal to price

   c. The marginal revenue (MR) should be equal to quantity

   d. None of the above

7. **Identify the correct statement:**

   a. Supernormal profit is normal profit plus the opportunity cost

   b. Opportunity cost is part of the normal profit

   c. Normal profit is obtained at the breakeven point

   d. The shutdown point is above the breakeven point

8. **The shutdown point is a point at which _____.**

   a. the opportunity cost is not covered

   b. the fixed cost is not recovered

   c. the variable cost is not recovered

   d. the firm stops production

9. **The breakeven point is a point at which the firm covers its _____.**

   a. variable costs

   b. fixed costs

   c. minimum average cost

   d. total cost

10. At the shutdown price:

   a. The fixed cost will be equal to the loss incurred by the firm

   b. The variable cost will be equal to the revenue

   c. Both a and b

   d. None of the above

Answers	1 – d	2 – a	3 – c	4 – d	5 – d
	6 – a	7 – b	8 – d	9 – c	10 – c

Chapter **9**

Theory of Factor Pricing

In this chapter, an overview of the theory of factor pricing is provided. Various inputs and their prices are important for any production system. The ultimate cost of goods depends on the prices of various factors of production. This chapter introduces the readers to the nature of factor demands. The chapter also explains the determinants of demand and supply of factors of production. It also gives the reader an introduction to the determination of factor prices.

The key learning objectives of this chapter include the reader's understanding of the following:

- Concept of factor pricing
- Nature of factor demand.
- Characteristics of demand of factors of production.
- Characteristics of supply of factors of production.
- Basic determinants of factor prices.

- Determination of factor prices through demand and supply.

- Determination of wages in a perfectly competitive market.

9.1 The Theory of Factor Pricing: An Overview

Land, labor, capital, and entrepreneurship are considered to be the factors of production. They are the main inputs for any production process. Factor prices are determined in the same way as the prices of consumer goods, i.e. by the interaction of supply and demand. There is no fundamental difference in price determination of factors and final products[73]. As the law of supply and demand determines the price of consumer goods, in the same way, factor prices are also determined. The prices of land, labor, capital, and entrepreneurship are called rent, wages, interest rate, and profit[74].

---

73. Ahuja, H. L. (2019). Advanced Economic Theory: Microeconomic Analysis.p.595 S. Chand Publishing

74. https://www.encyclopedia.com/finance/finance-and-accounting-magazines/factors-production

9.2 The Nature of Factor Demands

Derived Demand

While the demand for consumer goods is autonomous, the demand for factors of production is a derived demand[75]. The demand for factors depends on their productivity. Whatever the factors can produce must be in demand for the factors to have demand. Land, labor, or capital are in demand because they can produce goods and services that are demanded by the consumers[76]. Hence, the demand for factors is termed as derived demand. In the words of Samuelson and Nordhaus, "The firm's demand for inputs is derived indirectly from the consumer demand for its final product"[77]. Skilled labor and fertile land are demanded, according to their productivity.

Interdependent Demand

The factors of production are interdependent for their productivity. A farmer cannot plow the land without his tractor. A tailor cannot stitch garments without his or her sewing machine. All the factors are important for production and it is a difficult task to determine their relative importance. It is also usually impossible to calculate the contribution of a single input like labor or capital. The difficulty of separating the contribution of various

---

75. Dwivedi, D. N. (2016). Microeconomics: Theory and Applications.p.427. Vikas Publishing House.

76. Samuelson, P. A., & Nordhaus, W. D. (2009). Economics 19e.p 270

77. Samuelson, P. A., & Nordhaus, W. D. (2009). Economics 19e.p 233

factors makes the distribution of income a complex task[78]. If we could determine the specific contribution of land, the labor of the farmer, the tractor, fertilizer, or seeds in growing crops, we could easily distribute the income generated by the farm. But, in reality, it is a difficult proposition.

9.3 Marginal Revenue Product

Marginal Revenue of a product is the additional revenue produced by using an additional unit of input. Following Samuelson and Nordhaus[79], it can be explained as "Marginal revenue product represents the additional revenue a firm earns from using an additional unit of input, with other inputs held constant. It is calculated as the marginal product of the input multiplied by the marginal revenue obtained from selling an extra unit of output".

The above holds for all inputs. It can be written mathematically as

$MRP_L = MR \times MP_L$ where MRP_L is the marginal revenue product of labor

Or $MRP_c = MR \times MP_c$, where MRP_c is the marginal revenue product of capital

MR = Marginal Revenue

MP_L = Labor's Marginal Product

MP_c = Capital's Marginal Product

78. Samuelson, P. A., & Nordhaus, W. D. (2009). Economics 19e.p 234

79. Samuelson, P. A., & Nordhaus, W. D. (2009). Economics 19e.p 236

It can be extended to any input like land, entrepreneurship, etc.

In case of imperfect competition, the marginal product revenue is less than the price (MR < P), as the company has to reduce the price of previous units to sell the additional unit.

It is simpler in the case of perfect competition as the firm need not reduce its price for selling the additional unit. Here MR = P, hence,

$$MRP_{L,C} = P \times MP_{L,C}$$

Let's assume that the recruitment of an additional laborer increases the production of t-Shirts in a garment manufacturing company by 100 pieces. Each piece costs $5.

In the case of perfect competition,

$$MP_L = 5 \times 100 = \$ 500$$

But in the case of imperfect competition, the market price may go down to $4, and consequently, $MP_L = 4 \times 100 = \$400$

With the objective of profit maximization, firms will purchase inputs up to that point where $1 spent on inputs will produce output worth $1.

As per Salvatore[80], "For a firm to maximize its total profits, it must produce its best level of output with the best (least cost) input combination.."

These two conditions are satisfied when

$$MP_a/ P_a = MP_b /P_b = 1 \ MC_x = 1 /P_x$$

___
80. Salvatore, Dominick. Schaum's Outline of Microeconomics, 4th edition. McGraw-Hill, 2006.

where MP is the marginal product, P is the price, MC is the marginal cost; a and b are inputs, and x is the final product.

9.4 The Demand for Factors of Production

With the objective of profit maximization in mind, firms need to create an optimal combination of inputs. This combination leads to the demand for the factors of production.

Table 9.1	Marginal Revenue Product for perfectly competitive firms

Variable Factor (labor)	Total Product (T-shirts)	MRP$_L$ (Units)	Price of output ($ per T-shirt)	Marginal revenue product of labor (in $)
1	100	100	5	500
2	190	90	5	450
3	260	70	5	350
4	290	30	5	150
5	290	0	5	0

Let's consider the situation of a garment factory as depicted in Table 9.1. With one unit of labor, the profit-maximizing entity XYZ apparel earns a marginal revenue product of $500. Suppose the wages of the labor are $400 Then the profit of XYZ apparel is $ 100. When they recruit the second laborer the MRP is $450 but the company still makes a profit of $ 50. However, when they engage the third laborer, the profit becomes negative after paying the wage of $ 400 to the labor. The firm's operations remain profitable up till the recruitment of two laborers. Hence, the operations are viable up to the addition of two laborers. This way, the demand for labor and other inputs is decided. Profit earned per labor is the rationale behind determining the demand of the laborers. In the words of Samuelson and Nordhaus, "To maximize profits, firms should add inputs up to the point where the marginal revenue product of the input equals the marginal cost or price of the input."[81]

Figure 9.1

a. MRPL Curve in Quantity

MRPL (Units)

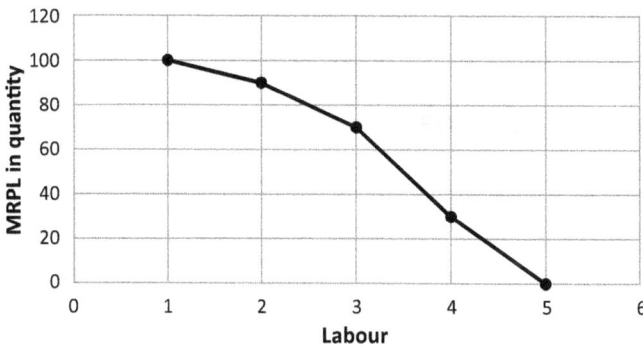

b. MRPL curve in $

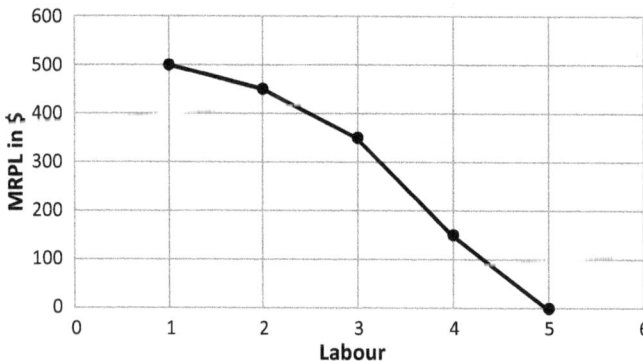

81. Samuelson, P. A., & Nordhaus, W. D. (2009). Economics 19e.p 237

A similar shape of the curve is seen in the marginal revenue productivity of the labor curve; quantity of goods produced and the value of the goods as the price per unit is constant. The curve slopes downward as total production increases but the revenue decreases at a diminishing rate when additional units of labor are employed. The MRPL curve provides the basis for the derivation of demand for a factor of production. The marginal revenue product schedule for each input gives the demand schedule of the firm for that input. So, the demand schedule of the labor can be derived from the MRPL schedule and the demand schedule of the capital can be derived from the MRPc schedule.

9.5 Supply of Factors of Production

Supply side of the factors of production needs to be analyzed along with the demand for the determination of factor prices. The supply of factors of production will vary from input to input. The determinants of supply will also be different for different inputs. The elasticity of the supply of the factors will also vary. Mostly, the supply of the inputs will have a positive slope towards the right. However, the land will remain inelastic. There can be negative slopes in the case of the supply of factors of production too. When the wage rate rises, some laborers may choose to work fewer hours.

The supply of labor is dependent on the wage rate and demography of the country. Samuelson[82] says, "The important determinants of labor supply are the price of labor (i.e., the wage rate) and demographic factors, such as age, gender, education,

---

82. Samuelson, P. A., & Nordhaus, W. D. (2009). Economics 19e.p 238

and family structure". A country with a younger population like India has a demographic dividend and an abundant supply of workers. Education increases the pull of skilled workers, as seen in South Korea and Japan. Factors like land depend on geological factors but their supply cannot be changed much. There can only be changes in their usage, like the conversion of wasteland into industrial land. Factors like capital investment are dependent on global interest rates, investment sentiments, country ratings, etc. The mobility of factors of production is also an important determinant of their supply. In perfect competition, the factors of production are mobile. Labor migration affects the wages and supply of labor. There can be migration of labor from underdeveloped countries to developed countries. Capital can also move with the expectation of higher returns.

9.6 Determination of Factor Prices through Demand and Supply

For determining factor prices, we need the market demand and supply for each of the inputs. Land, labor, and capital have individual demands for the firms operating in a market. When we add together the individual demand for the firms, we get the market demand. Let's assume that in the automobile industry in South Korea, there are four main players— Hyundai, Kia, GM-Korea, and Renault-Samsung. Now, the four companies require fresh graduate automobile engineers in 2022. Suppose, Hyundai has a requirement of 600, Kia-500, GM-500, and Renault - Samsung- 300 engineers. Then, the demand for graduate automobile engineers in South Korea will be 1900. Now, this has to equate with the supply of automobile engineers from Korean institutes and universities. If there is a shortage of supply, people from other countries may also be attracted by the industry. Based on the supply and demand, the companies can decide on the base level salaries. The intersection of the supply and demand curves will determine the price of the factors. According to Samuelson,[83] "The equilibrium price of the inputs in a competitive market is at that level where the quantities supplied and demanded are equal". The equilibrium point is shown in figure 9.2.

Figure 9.2 **Determination of factor prices based on derived demand and factor supply**

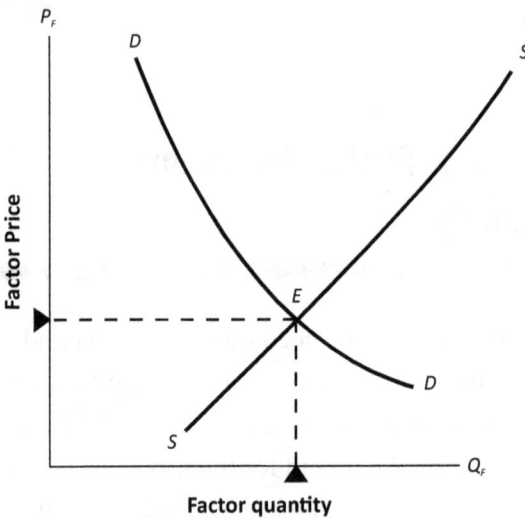

Factor quantity

The equilibrium point changes according to the change in supply or demand. If there is a growth in the automobile market, there will be an expansion in the production of various auto companies. If the supply of engineers does not increase immediately, there will be a rise in the salary level of fresh

---

83. Samuelson, P. A., & Nordhaus, W. D. (2009). Economics 19e.p 240

engineers. If the demand curve shifts to the right side due to the expansion of industry, the price point will shift upward. Again, if the supply reduces at a given price, then the supply curve will shift to the left, thereby increasing the price.

This interaction of demand and supply will take place for all factors of production, and accordingly prices will be determined.

For the convenience of discussion, we consider only two factors of production; labor and capital. The firm's labor demand curve is derived under two conditions:

a. When only the labor factor varies and capital remains constant

b. When both labor and capital are variable factors

In the short run, a firm may not be able to infuse capital, but in the long run, both capital and labor may vary. Due to the interdependence of factors, the derivation of the contribution of a single factor becomes difficult. Due to the interdependence of labor and capital, it is complicated to determine the contribution of a single factor. The problem becomes much more complicated when there are more than two factors. When one of the factors of production becomes cheaper, the other factor becomes relatively costlier. As profit-making entities, the firms try to substitute the cheaper factor for the costlier factor. This is called the substitution effect[84]. The substitution rule and derived demand are applicable in case of both perfect and imperfect competition in the product market.[85]

---

84. Dwivedi, D. N. (2016). Microeconomics: Theory and Applications.p.433. Vikas Publishing House.

85. Samuelson, P. A., & Nordhaus, W. D. (2009). Economics 19e.p 238

Discussion Questions

1. What are the different factors of production? Will there be any changes in the factors depending on the type of product? Justify with an example.

2. Write the various determinants of demand for factors of production.

Chapter Summary

◆ The ultimate cost of the goods depends on the prices of various factors of production.

◆ Land, labor, capital, and entrepreneurship are considered to be the factors of production.

◆ While the demand for consumer goods is an autonomous demand, the demand for factors is a derived demand.

◆ Demand for factors depends on their productivity.

◆ Factors of production are interdependent from their productivity. The productivity of labor is dependent on capital investments and vice versa.

◆ Marginal revenue of a product is the additional revenue produced by using an additional unit of input.

◆ In case of imperfect competition, the marginal product revenue is less than the price (MR < P), as the company has to reduce the price of previous units to sell the additional unit. In the case of perfect competition, the firm need not reduce the price for selling the additional unit.
Here, MR = P

◆ The elasticity of supply of various factors of production is different.

◆ The equilibrium price of an input is at the level where the supply of the factor is equal to the demand of the factor.

Quiz

1. **Derived demand is the demand based on the**

    a. demand of the final products which the factor can produce

    b. elasticity of demand

    c. taste and income of the buyer

    d. taste and income of the seller

2. **Identify the correct statement:**

    a. Autonomous demand is applicable for the inputs in production

    b. Derived demand is applicable for the consumer goods

    c. Autonomous demand and derived demand intersect each other

    d. Autonomous demand is applicable for the final products

3. **Marginal product is calculated as the product of the**

    a. price of the factor and demand for the factor

    b. demand for labor and wage rate

    c. marginal product and quantity

    d. marginal product and price of the product

4. **When the wage rate increases, the demand curve of labor will**

    a. shift to the left

    b. shift to the right

    c. does not shift but there is a movement along it

    d. will be in equilibrium

5. **Labor and capital vary in the**

    a. short run

    b. long run

    c. both cannot vary

    d. cannot be said

6. **Factors are interdependent because**

    a. their productivity depends on each other

    b. they are procured from the same market

    c. they are procured for the same industry

    d. the firms are interdependent

7. **The marginal revenue product MR is less than Price P in the case of**

    a. perfect competition

    b. imperfect competition

    c. only in case of monopolistic competition

    d. none of the above

8. In case of perfect competition, the slope of the marginal revenue product in in terms of units and marginal product revenue in terms of value ($) will be the same when

   a. the product price goes down

   b. the product price goes up

   c. the product price remains the same

   d. none of the above

9. The price of a factor is determined at a point where

   a. demand is equal to supply

   b. demand is above supply

   c. supply is more than demand

   d. none of the above

10. In imperfect competition, for selling an additional unit, the price of the previous units

   a. decrease

   b. increase

   c. remain same

   d. cannot be said

Answers	1 – a	2 – d	3 – d	4 – c	5 – b
	6 – a	7 – b	8 – c	9 – a	10 – a

Chapter **10**

International Trade

This chapter introduces the readers to the basics of international trade. The chapter deals with the rationale behind foreign trade and related theories. The chapter also outlines the theories of absolute advantage and comparative advantage and calculates the gains from trade in a two-country trading scenario. It further explains the demand and supply in international trade with instances of free trade and tariff protection. The demand and supply curves in international trade are drawn from the principles of microeconomic theories as explained in the initial chapters.

Key learning objectives of this chapter include the reader's understanding of the following

- The basic philosophy behind international trade

- Necessities for international trade

- Theory of absolute advantage

- Theory of comparative advantage

- Assumptions behind the theory of comparative advantage

- How the gains from trade are calculated in a two-country, two-products trading scenario

- Interaction of demand and supply curves in a free trade scenario

- How the equilibrium point is reached in case of an imposition of tariff

10.1 Basics of Foreign Trade

Globalization and trade between countries has changed the way the world eats, dresses, and even thinks. International trade has facilitated the supply of goods from one part of the world to the other. All natural resources are not available in all parts of the world. Furthermore, some of the countries are more competent in manufacturing some of the products. Now, even if Chinese farms do not produce kiwis, consumers can procure them from New Zealand. If better quality mangoes are available in India, Denmark can import them. Netflix or YouTube gives the world access to creative content produced in various corners of the globe. A student in Kenya can enroll in the courses offered by IVY league universities through Coursera or Edx if he or she has access to the internet. International trade ensures that people across the world receive a variety of goods and services at a cheaper cost, thus improving their quality of life.

Resource endowment is the basis of foreign trade. There are differences in resource endowments between countries. While some countries have abundant human capital, some countries are known for their technological prowess. Usually, no country will have all the resources needed by it within its boundary in a cost-effective manner and that is why international trade is imperative.

10.2 Reasons for International Trade

While primary reasons for international trade are the availability of resources and competencies in production, other reasons can be having diversity in natural resources due to geographical conditions, differences in tastes, and differences in costs.[86]

Diversity in Natural Resources

One country may be blessed with natural resources like petroleum or iron ore, another country may have excellent production chains of footwear while yet another country may have large amounts of fertile agricultural land. While India has large reserves of quality iron ore, China has an excellent production system of steel. It can import iron ore from India to manufacture steel for supplying to the world market. Cotton is grown in many countries which are exported to other countries for their textile industry.

86. Samuelson, P. A., & Nordhaus, W. D. (2009). Economics 19e.p 341

Differences in Taste or Culture

A country may sometimes prefer to export its natural resources or manufactured goods that are less popular in its domestic market but have more demand in international markets. These differences in taste or culture allow countries to opt for international trade, thus enhancing mutual benefits.

Differences in Cost

Some countries achieve economies of scale with large production volumes. We can see this in the case of many industries in China including electronic goods, garments, and steel. The large-scale production reduces the unit cost and makes exports feasible at a low cost. There is a huge difference in the labor cost from country to country. Countries like Sri Lanka, Indonesia, Vietnam, and Bangladesh have low labor costs and hence they have an advantage in producing footwear or garments which are labor-intensive industries. The consumers of developed countries benefit from these low-cost imports.

Integration of Value Chains

There are regional trade agreements like the USMCA (USA-Mexico-Canada Agreement), formerly the North American Free Trade Agreement (NAFTA), Regional Comprehensive Economic Partnership (RCEP), or Gulf Cooperation Council (GCC). The countries within these groupings have the benefit of producing at a low cost due to intra-industry trade between the countries. The countries which are part of these Regional Trade Agreements (RTAs) take advantage of the integration of the value chain and develop competency in exports.

10.3 Absolute Advantage

The theory of absolute advantage is credited to Adam Smith.[87] Marrewijk[88] puts it as "A country is said to have an absolute advantage over another country in the production of a good or service if it can produce that good or service using fewer real resources". So a country with an absolute advantage can produce more of an item using the same amount of inputs. In the words of Dwivedi,[89] "The theory of absolute advantage states that the basis of trade between the nations is the absolute advantage a country has in producing a commodity over the other countries." Based on this theory, we can say that China has an absolute advantage in producing toys over any other country like Japan. As China can produce more toys using the same amount of inputs, it will be rational for Japan to import toys from China rather than making it on its own soil. Now as per absolute advantage, countries will gain from trade as long as they have an absolute advantage in producing at least one good. Let's assume that China has an absolute advantage in producing toys and Japan has an absolute advantage in producing medicines. Let's hypothetically think that these two economies only make toys and medicines to survive. Spending all their resources on toys and medicines, China can produce 10x amount of toys and 5y amount of medicines in a year. Japan also produces 10x the amount of toys and 5y the amount of medicines. But we already know that China has an absolute advantage in making toys, so if the country concentrated only on making toys, it could produce 25x the amount of toys and zero

---

87. Smith, A. (1863). An Inquiry into the nature and causes of the Wealth of Nations.

88. van Marrewijk, J.G.M. (2008). Absolute advantage. Princeton University Press

89. Dwivedi, D. N. (2016). Microeconomics: Theory and Applications.p.578. Vikas Publishing House.

medicines. Similarly, by spending all resources like capital and labor on manufacturing medicines, Japan could make 20y more medicines.

Now, in a non-trade scenario, both the countries together can make 20x amount of toys and 10 y amount of medicines.

But when the countries agree to trade and start concentrating on their area of expertise, the total production of the toys will be 25x and medicines will be 20y. So the countries together enjoy 5x more toys and 10y more medicines.

But, suppose a country has an absolute advantage over the other in manufacturing both the products. Suppose, China or Japan is more competent in manufacturing both toys and medicines, then what will happen to international trade? Absolute advantage cannot answer this and here comes the theory of comparative advantage which is widely accepted till date.

10.4 Comparative Advantage

Following the theory of absolute advantage, we see that both countries could benefit when both had an advantage over the others on at least one commodity. The question is what would happen if a country has more competitiveness or advantages in producing both? English Economist David Ricardo[90] dealt with this question with two regions, the USA and Europe, and developed the theory of comparative advantage. As per the theory of comparative advantage, both the countries will still gain from

---

90. Ruffin, R. (2002). David Ricardo's discovery of comparative advantage. History of political economy, 34(4), 727-748.

trade as they will choose to trade on the item in which they have relatively more advantage. Samuelson and Nordhaus[91] write, "The principle of comparative advantage holds that each country will benefit if it specializes in the production and export of those goods that it can produce at a relatively low cost. Conversely, each country will benefit if it imports those goods which it produces at a relatively high cost."

Let's assume that Vietnam and Cambodia are two countries trading in pianos and pins. Vietnam can produce pianos at a cost of $1000 and pins at a cost of $1 per box. The cost of production in Cambodia for pianos and pins are $2000 and $1.5 respectively. Now, Vietnam has an absolute advantage in both commodities. However, it has comparatively more advantages in exporting pianos. It will mobilize all its resources for producing and exporting pianos and will prefer to import pins from Cambodia. This is the theory of comparative advantage which shows that trade is not expected to be unidirectional. Ricardo considered the costs of factors of production of commodities in his theory and this is based on the following assumptions:

a. It considered only one factor of production i.e. labor. The rest of the factors of production like land, capital, etc. were considered to be fixed or insignificant.

b. Labor across the world was taken as homogenous and differences in productivity were not considered

c. Supply of labor was taken as constant under the condition of full employment

d. Factors of production were considered to be mobile within the country but not between countries

---

91. Samuelson, P. A., & Nordhaus, W. D. (2009). Economics 19e.p 341

e. Value of a commodity and its exchange were based on labor cost

f. Logistics costs of exports were not considered

g. Non-tariff barriers between countries were considered

The theory of comparative advantage is considered to be the most acceptable theory of trade till date. In 1965, Balassa[92] developed an index called Revealed Comparative Advantage (RCA) which gives the measurement of comparative advantage based on the commodity's share in a country's export vis-a-vis its share in world trade. RCA is used widely for the measurement of the comparative advantage of various products of a country. Organizations like the International Trade Centre and World Bank maintain data of RCA for almost all countries across the world.

10.5 Gains from Trade

In order to understand the gains from trade for two countries that are engaged in trade, let's consider a hypothetical situation of trade between Australia and Indonesia. Let us assume that both countries manufacture wheat and cloth with a difference in cost. Table 10.1 refers to the cost of labor producing wheat and cloth in their respective countries.

---

92. Balassa, B. (1965). Trade liberalisation and "revealed" comparative advantage 1. The Manchester school, 33(2), 99-123.

| Table 10.1 | Per ton labor cost (Man hours) | |

Country	Wheat	Cloth
Australia	15	30
Indonesia	25	40

| Table 10.2 | Opportunity Cost of Wheat and Cloth | |

Country	Wheat	Cloth
Australia	15/30= 0.5 tons of Cloth	30/15 = 2 tons of wheat
Indonesia	25/40 = 0.63 tons of cloth	40/25 = 1.6 tons of wheat

Let's assume a situation of autarky[93] which means that both the countries produce both wheat and cloth and there is no export or import between the countries.

Under the barter system, the domestic exchange rate in both countries is calculated.

In the case of Australia:

1 ton of wheat = 0.5 tons of cloth

1 ton of cloth = 2 tons of wheat

In the case of Indonesia:

1 ton of wheat = 0.63 tons of cloth

1 ton of cloth = 1.6 tons of wheat

Now, let's withdraw the trade embargo and allow both countries to freely trade. In the case of free trade, as per the

---

93. Autarky is an economic system of self-sufficiency and limited trade

theory of comparative advantage, Australia will export wheat to Indonesia and import cloth from Indonesia, as its relative competitiveness is more in the case of wheat.

We will next calculate whether the countries gain in the case of free trade. But before that, we need to understand an important concept of international trade, i.e. Terms of trade. Terms of trade are the rate at which countries exchange their products. Samuelson and Nordhaus[94] described it as " The "real" terms at which a nation sells its export products and buys its import products. This measure equals the ratio of an index of export prices to an index of import prices". So, favorable terms of trade mean export prices from a country will be higher compared to import prices. Now whether the two countries, Indonesia and Australia, will gain from trade will depend on the ratio of their external exchange rate to the domestic exchange rate. If the external exchange rate is higher compared to the domestic exchange rate, the countries will gain from trade[95].

Table 10.3   **Gains from International Trade**

Country	Domestic exchange rate for wheat	External exchange rate	Gain from trade
Australia	1 TW = 0.5 TC	1 TR = 0.63 TC	0.13 TC
Indonesia	1 TC = 1.6 TW	1 TC = 2 TW	1 TW

TW = Tons of wheat, TC = Tons of cloth

When both the countries are in autarky, they exchange one commodity for the other. So, Australia can sacrifice 1 ton of wheat for 0.5 tons of cloth within the domestic market, but when they

94. Samuelson, P. A., & Nordhaus, W. D. (2009). Economics 19e.p 675

95. Dwivedi, D. N. (2016). Microeconomics: Theory and Applications.p.582. Vikas Publishing House

trade, they can get 0.63 TC in lieu of 1 TW. The net gain of cloth is 0.13 Ton cloth. Similarly, Indonesia can produce 1.6 tons of wheat instead of 1 ton of cloth, but when they begin exporting, they can import 2 tons of wheat in lieu of 1 ton of cloth, leading to a gain of 1 ton of wheat. So, following the theory of comparative advantage, both the countries gain.

10.6 Free Trade and Trade Barriers

Across the world there have been movements for the protection of domestic industries. Developed countries like the USA and Japan protected their market till 1970. Even today, there are concerns about China's exports to the USA and across the world. Despite the populist call for protectionism, free trade has an upper hand in bringing economic prosperity to the world. Economists are mostly unanimous in agreeing that free trade and the related gains from trade benefits consumers and finally the country's economy. However, calls for the protection of the domestic industry often lead to protectionist measures through tariff and non-tariff barriers. A tariff is a kind of tax that is imposed on an imported item from another country, raising its price in the importing country. This creates some advantages for the domestic industry. Though the principles of WTO propagate free trade and member countries extend the most favored nation status to each other with a commitment to keep tariffs lower, the WTO has achieved limited success so far. In figure 10.1 we analyzed a situation where Australia is a manufacturer of clothing as well as an importer in a free market. In figure 10.2, we find a situation where tariffs are imposed on the imported clothes.

| Figure 10.1 | Imports under Free Trade |

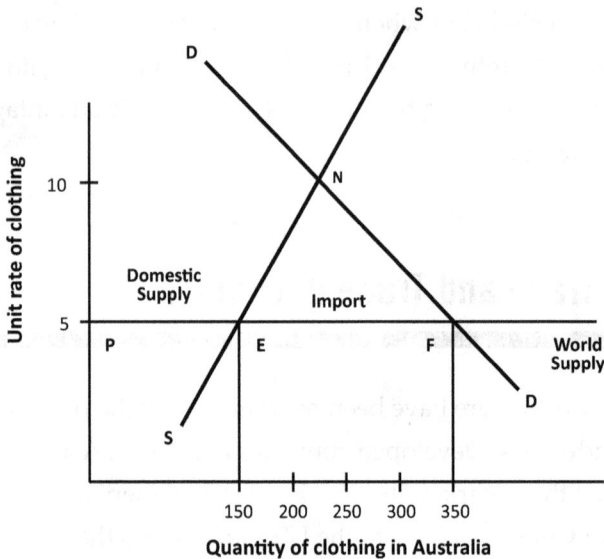

Quantity of clothing in Australia

The usual domestic demand curve and supply curve intersect each other at point N, determining the domestic price at $10. Now the supply of cloth worldwide is set at $5. In free trade conditions, goods from low-cost regions will flow toward high-cost regions and hence the world supply reaches Australia. Initially, without imports, the price was set at $10 and the demand and supply were at 200 units. Now, it is assumed that Australia's production quantity is so small that it hardly has any effect on the world price of cloth. When imports are allowed, the Australian price comes down to $5 and the new supply and demand are at 350, including 200 units of import. The world price is perfectly elastic and the supply curve is horizontal at $5. The new demand and supply intersect at point F, pushing the price down and increasing the consumption. This benefits the consumers in Australia. However, the quantity supplied by the local producers takes a hit.

Figure 10.2 **Imports when a tariff is imposed**

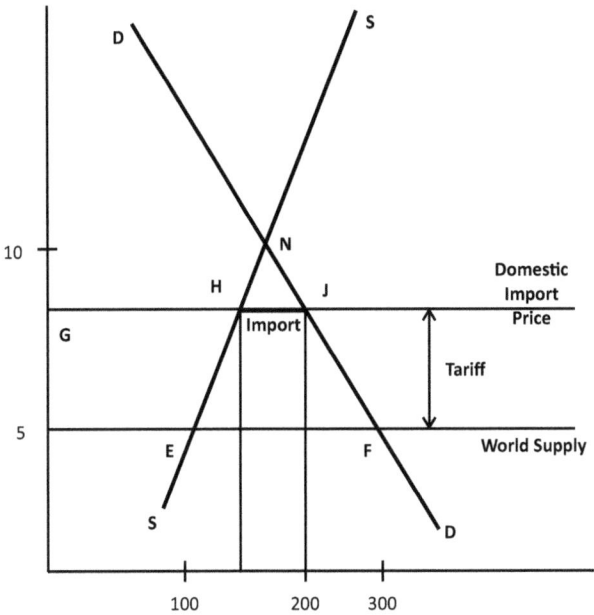

In figure 10.2, the initial demand and supply curves intersect each other at point N, the price point is at $10 and supply is at 150 units. Now a tariff of $3 is imposed on imports from other countries. The new price is set at $8 and the supply intersects the demand curve at point J, with HJ being the new import after the imposition of the tariff. If the tariff is increased more to the level of $5, then there will hardly be any import of cloth to the Australian market. The current tariff of $3 can be termed as a non-prohibitive tariff which is keeping room for some imports. However, if it is raised to $5, it will become a prohibitive tariff restricting all imports. While tariff barriers can be quantified, non-tariff barriers cannot be quantified. There are various restrictions imposed on imports, including clauses of health and safety, restricting imports with an upper limit or quota, restrictions on imports during some particular season, etc. which create impediments to free trade.

While gains from trade are established by various theories developed by economists, the world is yet to reach an era of unrestricted free trade and globalization. In reality, the process strives for lower tariffs and therefore, freer trade.

Discussion Questions

1. Imagine a hypothetical situation of trade between China and Japan. China has more advantages in exporting both toys and shoes to Japan. The gain from trade for toys per unit is $5 and shoes per unit is $2. Therefore, will China export both the commodities? Analyse the situation and answer by using Ricardo's theory of comparative advantage.

2. Trade leads to prosperity and welfare. Do you agree with this? How do non-tariff barriers affect free trade between countries?

Chapter Summary

◆ Resource endowment is the basis of foreign trade. There are differences in resource endowments between countries.

◆ The primary reasons for international trade are the availability of resources and competencies in production. Other reasons could be diversity in natural resources due to geographical conditions, differences in tastes, differences in cost, integration of the value chain, etc.

◆ Adam Smith's theory of absolute advantage says that a country has an absolute advantage over another country in the production of a good or service if it can produce that good or service using fewer real resources.

◆ As per the theory of comparative advantage of Ricardo, in case a country has an absolute advantage over another in both the traded goods, both the countries will still gain from trade as they will choose to trade on the item in which they have a greater relative advantage.

◆ The theory of comparative advantage considers only one factor of production, i.e. labor, and a scenario with no tariff barrier.

◆ Revealed Comparative Advantage (RCA) is the measurement of comparative advantage based on the commodity's share in a country's export vis-a-vis its share in world exports.

◆ Terms of trade are the rate at which countries exchange their products. It is the ratio of an index of export prices to an index of import prices.

- ◆ The gains from trade of countries are dependent on the terms of trade.

- ◆ In the case of free trade, domestic prices follow world prices.

- ◆ In the case of tariffs, the domestic price will be the world price plus tariffs.

- ◆ Tariffs can be prohibitive and non-prohibitive.

Quiz

1. **Countries gain from international trade because**

    a. the demand structure varies from country to country

    b. all natural resources are not available in all countries

    c. all countries are not equally competent in manufacturing all goods and services

    d. b and c

2. **The theory of absolute advantage states that a country will export goods in which**

    a. it has a cost advantage

    b. which are advantageous for its national policy

    c. in which it wants to build a competency

    d. none of the above

3. **The theory of comparative advantage shows that countries export the items in which**

    a. they have cost advantages

    b. they have relative cost advantages

    c. they have quality advantages

    d. none of the above

4. The theory of absolute advantage is credited to

a. David Ricardo

b. Paul Samuelson

c. Adam Smith

d. Karl Marx

5. Gains from trade depend on

a. absolute advantage of a country

b. comparative advantage of a country

c. terms of trade

d. Options b and c

6. Terms of trade is the ratio of

a. export volume to import volume

b. an index of export value to an index of import value

c. an index of export volume to an index of import volume

d. an index of import value to an index of export value

7. Prohibitive tariff is a tariff

a. which makes the market price equal to or more than the market price in a non-trade scenario

b. which prohibits entry of imported goods

c. equal to the prevailing VAT in a country

d. none of the above

8. Non-prohibitive tariff is

a. non-tariff barrier

b. prohibitive tariff minus domestic price

c. domestic price plus tariff

d. a tariff that lowers the domestic price compared to the price in a no trade scenario, even after imposition of tariff.

9. The theory of comparative advantage takes into consideration the

a. price of capital

b. price of labor

c. both of the above

d. none of the above

10. When a non-prohibitive tariff is imposed on a good, the supply curve intersects the demand curve

   a. at a lower point compared to a situation of no-trade

   b. at a higher point compared to a situation of free trade

   c. at the same point

   d. both a and b

Answers	1 – d	2 – a	3 – b	4 – c	5 – d
	6 – b	7 – a	8 – d	9 – b	10 – d

Notes